Dedicated to my precious Max,
always in my mind and heart,
never to be forgotten.

INTRODUCTION

We lost Max, our firstborn son, on June 3, 2020, to suicide, after a long and difficult battle with depression. What you are now holding is essentially my diary entries from the first eighteen months following his death. As I tried to process the devastating loss we'd experienced, journaling allowed me to put my swirling thoughts and emotions into words, not an easy task by any means.

My grief journey has been messy, desperate, and chaotic. As you read through the reflections I've written in the following pages, you will see the same emotions surface again and again. Things like hopelessness, anger, guilt, regret, apathy, and more will be mentioned over and over as these emotions consumed me in the days, weeks, and months following Max's passing. Going through such a catastrophic loss is anything but linear and predictable, but more on that later in the book.

As a follower of Jesus, I found myself at a critical juncture in my faith. I've tried to be honest about the serious doubts and questions I entertained throughout. I believe many of us experience a crisis of faith at some point in our lives, and I've attempted to portray mine with authenticity and humility.

I know these reflections may be painful and difficult to read, but I've tried to balance the heavy content with the beauty of the artwork from my fabulously talented designer and illustrator, Sarah Nelsen. Such is life—the juxtaposition of beauty and pain. You may not have experienced the loss of a child, but I believe my unexpected and unpredictable journey will speak to you as you navigate your own loss. I pray this book will bring clarity and comfort to you.

FOREWARD

We know little

We can tell less

But one thing I know

One thing I can tell

I will see you again in Jerusalem

By Anne Porter

You hold a very special book in your hands. The words that fill it were borne of deep sorrow and heartbreak. These words are the exact words the author had hoped and prayed to never write. And yet, when forced to write them, she also decided to courageously open the doors of her private grief with the hope that someone would read her words and feel less alone.

Who is the author? She's a wife to Bill and a mother to Max and Sam. She's a dog owner, a fellow book lover, a terrific gardener, and a fantastic cook. She's someone who loves to travel, someone who loves a big dinner party, someone whose door is always open, and someone her friends can count on. She shows up, she listens, and she cares. She's my beautiful and heartbroken best friend, Erin.

The life that Erin is living now is not the one she envisioned. The life she lives now is the life she fought like hell to prevent. However, it is the life she is learning how to live. And the one she is sharing with us all, her readers. As you read Erin's reflections, my hope is that her transparency will help to tear down our culture's expectations of what grief should look like. My hope is that what she has discovered, and bravely shared, will offer a safe and grace-filled environment in which anyone on a similar path may find some acceptance.

For those of us who are walking alongside our loved ones as they grieve, there is much to learn from Erin's words. My own understanding of grief, courage, strength, sorrow, and faith have been expanded as I've watched my courageous friend fight to survive her immense loss. And she's taught me that the most important thing I can do for her, or anyone grieving, is to pray and be present. Words lifted to Jesus on her behalf have more power than anything else. Being present in her pain, in all the various forms it takes, is the only other thing she needs from those who love her. In that way, we are caring for her, and for others who grieve, just as Jesus cares for us.

Julie Boynton

TABLE OF CONTENTS

the first week

DAY ONE

June 3, 2020. The day our world was shattered into a million pieces. The day we got the call no parent ever wants to get. It was about 7:45 am, and I was still in bed when I noticed three missed calls from a former co-worker. Because I had not spoken to her in a couple of years, I thought, "How strange." I later found out one of Max's neighbors knew her and had called her to tell her about the emergency vehicles at Max's house, and she was trying to alert me.

Seconds later, my husband, Bill, burst into the room, crying, "Max is gone!" I remember thinking, "Gone where?" We then began the daunting task of calling family and friends to share the news. We started every conversation with "We lost Max," as if we could find him again if we tried. We could not say he "died" or, even worse, "took his own life." That would be too harsh, too real, too much to handle.

Within hours our house was full of people. First, our pastors arrived to pray with us. They recommended we welcome friends and family into our home for the next few days. They suggested we allow people to bring food, to come to sit with us, pray with us, and stay with us. They said the people who loved us would want to show their love tangibly, so we

"...as if we could find him again if we tried."

should permit it. I honestly did not know that was customary. I remember thinking, "Don't these people have to work?" It was a Wednesday afternoon.

Looking back, those first few days were a blur. We were numb with shock. It was like a bad dream.

Having all those people around our house was what got me out of bed each day. Their presence gave me the motivation to get up, get dressed, and eat. I doubt I would have done any of those things without them.

I am thankful for a loving and faithful community. Family and friends who were willing to show up, hug us, pray with us, cry with us, and, in some cases, literally hold us up. I am thankful we had that support system in place before the bottom dropped out because I doubt we would have survived otherwise.

DAY TWO

The day Max passed, I was sitting outside with a friend. She was heartbroken. I was numb. She kept saying, "I'm so mad at him! How could he do this to you?" She had lost a son herself, so she was intimately familiar with what I was, and would continue to be going through.

Three different times, after repeating her anger and distress, small twigs fell from the trees and onto her head. We have many oak trees on our property, so there is no shortage of twigs, leaves, and other tree debris.

Each time I would say to her, "See, he doesn't want you to be mad at him. He loves you! He was suffering and he thought it was his only way out. Please don't be angry with him!"

As the day went on, I noticed a bird in the bush nearby. The bird seemed to be trying to get my attention. He seemed to be watching me. The bird appeared the next day in the backyard as I sat on our screen porch. He fluttered and squawked from a nearby bush. I began to think perhaps it was sent by Max.

A couple of months later, my husband and I attended an outdoor worship event at the home of some friends. One of the speakers talked about his young adult son who suffered

"In the midst of intense sorrow, the bird was a little beacon of hope."

from serious health issues. He told us that he and his wife had been praying for healing for years. He described the heartache of believing and knowing God could heal their son, but not experiencing the healing. Boy, could we relate! At that event, my bird reappeared. He perched on the roof of their house for the duration of the event. In the midst of intense sorrow, he was a little beacon of hope.

Several people have since told me it is very common to have a similar encounter with a bird following the death of a loved one. They say it is a "sign" our loved one is close by and watching over us. I don't know if that's true, but I hope "my bird" continues to return to me as a reminder of my beautiful son.

DAY THREE

Our friends have been a tremendous blessing. They showed up before we even realized we needed them. A dear friend came from out of state and stayed with us for two weeks. She was my rock. She put me to bed when I needed to sleep, arranged to get medication to help me sleep when I could not, coordinated food for the throngs of people who continued to arrive each day, took my wine glass from my hand when I had had too much, and so much more.

"She was my rock."

One of the kindest things she did was to read a book on how to walk alongside a grieving parent. She suggested that other friends read it as well. What a powerful demonstration of love from these beautiful women, who would invest their time to read a book just to understand how best to love and support me during my greatest pain. That is true friendship. That is true love. That is true sacrifice. "There is no greater love than to lay down one's life for one's friend." John 15:13 (NLT)

"There is no greater love than to lay down one's life for one's friend."

- John 15:13 (NLT)

DAY FOUR

Max's roommate was the one to find him on June 3rd. He called 911, and the police and coroner arrived at their house. Although we spoke with the detective, we were not required to identify his body. This was a blessing.

Max was an organ donor, so we were contacted by CORE about the organs they would be collecting. It was difficult to process that our son's organs would be harvested for others, but we were ultimately thankful that his death would mean life for other people with serious health conditions. If only that had been a possibility for him.

"I felt a strong compulsion to see my sweet boy one last time."

"Denial is enticing and powerful."

After everything was complete, his body was transferred to the funeral home. Max wanted to be cremated, but the funeral home asked if we wanted to see him before that took place. I felt a strong compulsion to see my sweet boy one last time.

It was awful. He didn't look like himself. I remember touching him and crying, "He's so cold!" I could not reconcile his cold, lifeless body with the funny, witty, snarky, sensitive, loyal, compassionate, and brave person he was.

Looking back, I am glad I saw him because it brought a bit of closure I would not have had otherwise. Denial is enticing and powerful. If I had not seen him, my mind may have settled comfortably in denial of his absence.

DAY FIVE

Since Max passed, he has repeatedly appeared in my dreams. I have heard this often happens after losing someone you love. I am so very thankful for these "visits."

Sometimes in my dreams, we talk, and other times I just see him from afar. I like the ones where we talk best. I so enjoyed conversing with my beautiful boy in life. He was a serious talker.

When he was little, he made EVERYTHING talk—his cars, stuffed animals, action figures, and even forks and spoons. He started talking at twelve months, speaking in full sentences at fifteen months, and never stopped. We talked about everything, and I treasure those conversations. Well, I treasure most of them anyway.

Max was never at a loss for words. As a child, we could ask him question after question and never stump him. Max had an answer for everything. Our next-door neighbor used to play a game with him in which he would continually ask questions just to see what kind of story Max would come up with. His preschool teacher pulled me aside one day to ask if we were personal friends with the Pittsburgh Steeler, Jerome Bettis. She said Max talked about Jerome coming to our house for dinner so regularly and naturally that she assumed we knew him. He was creative and imaginative.

Max had strong opinions about everything. We knew where he stood on various issues, and he often challenged us to explore our positions by offering a new and different perspective. He was intelligent, thoughtful, and inquisitive, and he encouraged us to be as well.

Some people say that when Max appears in my dreams he is visiting me from Heaven to let me know he's okay. He's letting me know that he is always with me, and I don't have to be sad. I don't know if any of that is true. Perhaps I just miss him so desperately that I conjure him in my dreams to keep him close.

"...he is visiting me from Heaven to let me know he's okay."

DAY SIX

Planning a child's memorial service is not something any parent should ever have to do. Writing a child's obituary is a gruesome task. Delivering a child's eulogy is a heart-wrenching exercise.

We had the dubious distinction of holding both visitation at the funeral home and Max's memorial service during the 2020 COVID pandemic. The pandemic seemed to have little impact on the visitation, as hundreds of family members, friends, co-workers, neighbors, and acquaintances came to the funeral home to offer their condolences. Many of them talked about a family member who also struggled with depression or another form of mental illness. Conversely, many who came through the visitation line could not even speak. We were the walking epitome of every parent's worst nightmare, and it was almost too much for some people to bear.

The following week, the memorial service was limited to family due to COVID restrictions. Our church holds about 500 people, but we had fewer than 100 in attendance. As an alternative for other friends and family, who could not attend, we live-streamed the service. The service is still online, and to date, more than 1,000 people have viewed it.

"We must end the stigma."

Bill and I both spoke during the memorial service. I am so thankful I had the desire and fortitude to do so. During my eulogy, I tried to give others a glimpse of how special Max was. I talked about his talents and gifts, as well as his struggles. I tried my best to honor my precious son. He was one of the most intelligent, gifted, interesting, and yet troubled people I knew.

I didn't fully understand his mental illness. As a matter of fact, I could not even ascribe that label to him. I used to say he suffered from "mental health issues" rather than mental illness. Those words, "mental illness," seemed too scary, too permanent, and too serious.

There remains a stigma around mental illness. I think one reason is that some types of mental illness can be particularly scary and confusing. I understand this, but are we afraid of someone with diabetes, heart disease, or cancer? Of course not. We must end the stigma and treat mental illness with the same compassion, understanding, and empathy as we do physical illnesses. My boy deserved more understanding and compassion than he experienced in this life. My prayer is that others, who struggle as he did, will be treated better.

DAY SEVEN

Max left us a gift: his sweet dog, Emmy. She is a Border Collie/Lab mix and is the sweetest, most intuitive dog I have ever met. Like Max, she has her issues. She was rescued off the streets as a puppy and consequently has a serious anxiety disorder. She and Max were a good pair.

"...a place to direct my love for my son."

We got her for Max in September 2016 for his birthday. We thought the responsibility of taking care of a dog would be good for him. We thought she could be a companion and a therapy dog of sorts. He loved her deeply.

Emmy

"...grief is nothing but love with nowhere to go."

Since Max died, we share custody of Emmy with Bridget, Max's girlfriend. Having Emmy is like having a little piece of Max with us still. She gives me, and, I suspect, Bridget something to care for and love in lieu of him. I have heard that grief is nothing but love with nowhere to go. Emmy gives me a place to direct my overflowing love for my son.

the first month

THE FIRST MONTH

ENTRIES NO.1 + 2

Guilt. Regret. Anger. Shame. Sadness. Hopelessness. These are my companions now. Sometimes the feelings are so overwhelming I feel like I cannot breathe. I have never been particularly good at feeling my feelings. Instead, I ignore them or repress them and numb myself. Busyness can be a good distraction; so, can a good book. Since losing Max though, it has become easy to reach for a glass of wine to take the edge off and not have to feel my feelings. However, one glass can quickly become three. I am trying to take steps to not spiral out of control, but sometimes numbness feels better than anything else.

"...so overwhelming I feel like I cannot breathe."

Shortly after Max passed, different groups of friends approached us about giving us gifts in his memory. We were given two trees, a bench, a plaque, an engraved boulder, a garden art pole, and various plants. Thus, a memorial garden was born.

"...something tangible to do with my grief."

Gardening has always been therapeutic for me. I find it meditative and rewarding to work with my hands to help bring out the beauty of God's creation. Creating the Max Memorial Garden was particularly helpful because it gave me something tangible and physical to do with my grief.

It turned out exactly as I envisioned. It is a beautiful and peaceful reminder of my Max. He loved our property and the woods surrounding our home. He used to joke that I loved my plants more than I loved him and Sam. It feels right to have a special place on our property, where I can sit to reflect and remember him.

A Celebration of Life in Photos

the garden

"It feels right to have a special place on our property, where I can reflect and remember him."

"The Lord bless you and keep you;
The Lord make His face to shine upon you
and be gracious to you; the Lord turn
his face toward you and give you peace."

- Numbers 6:24-26

Do all things with love,
grace, and gratitude.

THE FIRST MONTH

ENTRY NO. 3

In the weeks following Max's death, I became more aware of how much he had struggled and suffered. Several of his friends, roommates, and neighbors shared things with us that we hadn't previously known, things that were quite painful and difficult to hear.

One of the hardest things we have ever had to do was pack up his possessions from his home. He had a bag filled with medications—ones he was currently taking and others that he had tried with little success in the unrelenting effort to control his depression and seizures from epilepsy. It was heartbreaking to me that our sweet boy had to deal with such serious health issues. A friend used to say, "Max is operating above his pay grade." He had so much more on his plate than many of his peers, and he was acutely aware of his differences.

I prayed for him for years. I so desperately wanted him to be cured of his many health issues. I believe in a God who can and does heal people, and I desperately wanted healing for my son. I wanted him to be delivered from his trials and his pain.

I once heard that God delivers us in one of three ways: *from the fire, through the fire, or by the fire*. From the fire refers to when God removes us from the trial to **build** our faith, as when

"I once heard that God delivers us...from the fire, through the fire, or by the fire."

a serious health issue is miraculously healed. Through the fire refers to when we experience the trial for a period of time, but ultimately God brings us *through* it safely to **refine** our faith. For example, this occurs when a serious health issue is brought under control, perhaps due to medication or intervention. By the fire refers to when He removes us from the trial and into His loving arms *by* way of death to **perfect** our faith.[1]

Although it saddens me, our Max was delivered *by his fire*. I cling to the belief that he is with Jesus and is no longer sad or suffering. My boy does not have to deal with the struggles that plagued him in this life anymore. I am immensely grateful for this.

platitudes

ENTRY NO. 4

Shortly after losing Max, I started reading a book written by a man who had lost his young son. His wife discovered their little boy had died in his bed. When she called her husband to tell him the news, his response was, "Jesus is still risen." I wanted to throw the book across the room.

It's not that I disagree with his statement, just the context. If anyone had said that to me upon hearing about Max's death, let alone my husband, I would have punched him in the face.

I have little tolerance for people who over-spiritualize what has happened. They try to wrap things up in a nice bow. They offer platitudes when NOTHING can explain what has happened. God forbid people use Bible verses to justify what we are going through. Death sucks. Suicide sucks even more because it is sudden, traumatic, and filled with "what ifs."

Nothing is more hurtful than when well-intentioned people try to explain, rationalize, or spiritualize Max's death. I've heard that the best thing to do when someone is going through a trial is to "show up and shut up." Sounds about right to me.

"...the best thing to do when someone is going through a trial is to show up and shut up."

ENTRY NO. 5

"...when I express anger because I have lost my precious son, I hope to receive grace."

Anger is an easy emotion. I have heard that it's the one we most often go to when the feelings swirling below the surface are just too painful. I agree. Furthermore, I find it really easy to project my anger onto a person or situation.

I've probably scared my friends to death. For years, my mantra has been "People say stupid *@^#." And that was just when Max was struggling. Now that he is gone, I am hyper-alert and easily offended by what people say. I really try not to lash out, but it's hard. I feel a great need to point out someone's insensitivity. When I do lash out, I'm hopeful people will forgive me. It is a tough thing to lose your son, your firstborn.

Max was one of the most fascinating people I have ever known, and I don't say that because I am his mom. He really was. He was intelligent and creative. He wrote poetry and songs. He did stand-up comedy. He was also an activist, often intervening on behalf of those he felt were marginalized or disadvantaged. I am immensely proud to be his mom.

So, when I express anger because I have lost my precious son, I hope to receive grace.

worry

THE FIRST MONTH

ENTRY NO. 6

Max struggled for years before he died. As a child, he was sensitive, dramatic, and anxious. In high school, he suffered from gastro-intestinal issues with no diagnosed medical cause. In college, he suffered from depression and anxiety/panic attacks. From the ages of eighteen to twenty-five, he was hospitalized five times for suicide ideation. Our local psychiatric hospital is a scary and depressing place. It broke my heart that my sweet boy felt he needed to check himself into it to keep himself safe.

But the last straw was when he was diagnosed at nineteen with epilepsy. Watching my sweet boy have a seizure was the most traumatic thing I have ever witnessed. Bill and I worried about him for years. We worried about his mental health and his physical health. We were afraid he would hurt himself, intentionally, due to his depression, or unintentionally due to a seizure. He sustained several injuries from seizures, including but not limited to a chipped tooth, a concussion, and a laceration requiring stitches.

"...the monster was finally out from under the bed."

We received many crisis calls from him, and we lived on high alert for a long time, always afraid of the worst. But the call we feared the most was that he had left us, that he was gone.

When "the call" finally came, it was as if the monster was finally out from under the bed. In addition to the shock and helplessness, there was a sense of relief. Relief that we would get no more crisis calls, have no more gut-wrenching worry or sleepless nights wondering about Max and his future.

Obviously, with the sense of relief came feelings of guilt. Again, we thought, "What kind of parents are we?" I keep hearing that it's important to feel my feelings, to just sit with them without judgment. I seriously don't know how to do that! As soon as a feeling surfaces, I judge it as either a good or bad feeling. Doesn't everybody do this?

A good friend of mine lost her son more than ten years ago. Her advice and support have been invaluable. Hearing her say, "He was your worry," has allowed me to admit that it's a relief to no longer live with the worry that plagued me for eight years. Her reassurance that my feelings of relief are normal and understandable has been incredibly helpful. Sometimes when someone else validates my feelings, it helps me be a little kinder to myself.

the first year and a half

JULY THROUGH OCTOBER

Habit and memory seem to keep your body moving in the right direction even when you aren't aware.

A couple of months after losing Max, a friend gave me a journal on self-care. I thought, "Self-care. That's an oxymoron." When you lose a child, self-care becomes a foreign concept. Why on earth would I care about myself when I have just lost my son? How could I possibly care about myself when my world has just been shattered? I simply had no desire or motivation to care for myself. I felt like I was going through the motions of life, and at times I still do. Things like getting out of bed, dressing in the morning, showering, and even eating were things I did by rote. I was only able to do them because I've done them so many times before. Habit and memory are funny things, as they seem to keep your body moving in the right direction even when you aren't conscious of your actions.

Those first couple of months after Max died and the COVID pandemic continued to rage around us, I remember thinking, "A diagnosis wouldn't be the worst thing." I thought, "I don't care if I get sick." While driving I would think, "An accident would be okay." I felt apathy, despair, and a sense of recklessness.

It's not that I don't have other people to love and live for. I am incredibly blessed to have a strong marriage with my husband, Bill, a close relationship with my son, Sam, and a wonderful, supportive group of extended family and friends. It is just that I felt such a hole in my heart, I wasn't sure I wanted to go on like that. Those feelings have diminished a bit, but there are still days I think about how good it would feel to be with Max again now. I know it will happen one day. I know I will hug and kiss him again.

One of my favorite pictures of Max and me is from our marriage vow renewal in 2017. I am holding his face in my hands and leaning in to give him a kiss. His eyes are closed, and he has the sweetest little smile on his face. That look is exactly the one he used to have as a little boy when I would kiss him. This cherished photo is a beautiful reminder of our strong bond and love for each other.

Trusted friends are a gift and, as I am starting to realize, so was every day I had with my sweet Max.

I have read several books about loss, death, and grief since losing Max. A common theme is to be thankful we had our loved one for as long as we did. The sentiment is that every day is or was a gift. I struggle with that idea. We had him for such a brief time, and he suffered so much during his short life.

We have a photo of Bill and me when I was about seven months pregnant with Max. I am wearing a peach-colored jumpsuit, and I look like an Easter egg. Bill is behind me, resting his chin on my shoulder, and we both have our hands on my belly. Our faces are filled with love and hope.

As I have looked at that photo since losing Max, I've thought, "If I'd known before getting pregnant that we'd only have him for twenty-five years, would I still have wanted him?" As painful as it is to admit, I am not sure. As if that admission is not painful enough, the very question fills me with tremendous guilt. What kind of mother would not want her child regardless of how much time she might have with him? *continued on next page*

That is a recurring thought, "What kind of mother would (fill in the blank)?" There have been times when the guilt is overwhelming. Thank goodness for supportive friends who have assured me that such thoughts do not mean I am, or was, a terrible mother. Trusted friends are a gift, and, as I am starting to realize, so was every day I had with my sweet Max.

Accepting that his intelligence, potential, and promise will not be fully realized in this life is a bitter pill to swallow.

Since losing Max, we've had friends who have experienced losses in their lives, such as pets, parents, other family members, relationships, businesses, and jobs. They have looked to us for sympathy. I truly don't mean to sound callous, but in the big scheme of things, losing a child trumps it all. I know it's not a competition, but when someone complains to me about 2020 being a "tough year," my sympathy deserts me. When someone cries about losing their dog, I want to say, "Try losing your son!" When someone laments the loss of their eighty-three-year-old aunt, I want to scream, "At least she led a long, full life!"

One of the hardest things to accept is that Max's life was cut so short. Accepting that his intelligence, potential, and promise will not be fully realized in this life is a bitter pill to swallow. I am choosing to believe his talents are being fully utilized in Heaven. It's the only way I can accept their absence here on Earth.

I do not know how to go through what we've been through and not ask "Why?"

When Max and his cousin, Michael, were thirteen, they made movies called "Boy vs. Backyard." They were based upon the TV show, *"Man vs. Wild."*[2] In the show, a former British SAS serviceman and survivalist would be dropped into a remote area and could rely only on his strength, stamina, and "know-how" to survive. My boys were captivated by this premise. Max and Michael made their own version with Max in the leading role and Michael as the cameraman.

They filmed an episode in my parent's carriage home neighborhood, on a cold January day. Max improvised for thirty minutes, deeming construction retention ponds "suitable drinking water," determining bumper stickers on vehicles were proof of a "cold climate," and declaring drive-by cars as "indigenous creatures." Our boy was remarkably creative. He was filled with promise and potential.

Hearing his young voice on this video before it changed is bittersweet. Watching this video before all his health issues began is almost too much to bear. Seeing this video now, knowing what was about to come, is so disheartening. It begs the question, Why? Why Max? Why our family? Why did he have to deal with depression, anxiety, AND epilepsy? I don't know how to go through what we've been through and not ask "Why?" Can others really do that? Are they being truthful?

One of the nicest things anyone said to me after he passed was, "You fought like hell for him."

By the grace of God, we have not been consumed with guilt for things left unsaid to Max. I am so thankful that our sweet boy did not pass when our relationship was riddled with angst as it was in earlier years. Because we had been through so much for so long with Max, we had said the things that needed to be said to one another. We had worked through many of the challenges and issues we had faced with him over the years. We had a strong, loving, and respectful relationship with him before he died.

One of the nicest things anyone said to me after he passed was, "You fought like hell for him." I did. Not always perfectly, God knows, but persistently and faithfully. I saw qualities and promise in him that he did not or could not see in himself, and I often pointed those things out to him. His intelligence, sense of humor, resilience, strength, and courage were remarkable to me, and I made sure he knew that.

Yet regret has crept into my mind and heart, regret about what more I could have done or done differently, and about things I should or should not have said. One of my biggest regrets is that I couldn't get into his "pit" with him.

One of his therapists told Bill and me that we shouldn't try to "fix" Max. We shouldn't try to reach into the pit he was in and try to pull him out. Instead during one of his depressive episodes, we should get into the pit with him. I simply couldn't do this.

"By the grace of God, we have not been consumed with guilt for things left unsaid..."

When he was in one of his depressive episodes, I would become so uncomfortable that I would think of ANY excuse to just get him out of bed. I remember one time dragging him around Target like a zombie. On this occasion and many others, I regret not climbing into bed with him and simply holding him. I regret not telling him I loved him and that he could and would get through the episode.

When he was a baby and he needed to be soothed, he would lie down and say, "Mommy, wipe mine back." I wish I had "wiped" his back when, as an adult, he needed my love and comfort the most.

Parenting is perhaps the best way to understand God. He loves us unconditionally.

Another video we've watched since Max's passing was one he made with cousin, Michael, at my parent's 70th birthday party, in 2008. They walked around interviewing party guests and asking, "What do John and Anita mean to you?" They were professional and adorable.

At the party, my sister, brother, and I all spoke to pay tribute to our parents. I was so struck by my words in the video. I talked about parenting like I actually knew what I was talking about. At the time, Max was thirteen and Sam was ten. Bill and I had been told repeatedly "what good parents you are," and we had believed it. We actually thought we had parenting all figured out, and I spoke with confidence and, if I'm honest, a bit of arrogance. If I had known the kind of humbling we would be facing in a short number of years, perhaps I would have changed the content of my speech.

I'm trying not to be too hard on myself. At that time, I honestly thought if I followed a certain formula, I would get a certain

continued on next page

outcome. How naïve! I fooled myself into thinking I had more control than I actually did, and it set me up for a hard fall.

Parenting is perhaps the best way to understand God. He loves us unconditionally. He doesn't force us to conform to His will. He loves us enough to allow us to make our own choices, even when those choices are not what's best for us. He allows us to make our own decisions, even when those decisions separate us from Him. HE is a good parent, and perhaps we would all do well to better follow His example.

Memories are precious.

One of my favorite things to do is reminisce about Max. A friend recently sent me a text remembering a time he was showing off a tattoo he had gotten on his birthday.

Leading up to his eighteenth birthday, he began to research tattoos. At eighteen he would be old enough to get one without parental consent, and he was fully committed to doing so. As an avid Star Wars fan, he selected an iconic symbol, the Millennium Falcon, for what would be his first of many tattoos.

On his eighteenth birthday, he not only got the tattoo but bought cigarettes and other items I shall not name. He was desperate to be an adult, but in equal measures, terrified. I think deep down he doubted he had the independence and resilience needed in adulthood. Oh, how wrong he was! Our boy had so very much to deal with, and he did so with courage and grit. We were so proud of him and wished he had been able to see in himself what we saw in him.

Sometimes people are reluctant to share with me a memory they have of Max. They're afraid they will remind me that he is gone. I am painfully aware of his passing every minute of every day. Despite this, I still like to remember the good and even not-so-good times we had with him. Memories are precious.

"I do believe; help my unbelief!"

"The Lord bless you and keep you; the Lord make His face shine on you and be gracious to you; the Lord turn His face toward you and give you peace." Numbers 6:24-26 (NIV)

These verses hold special meaning. I prayed them daily for years as our sweet Max battled his various health issues. I fervently prayed EVERY day for blessing, grace, and peace for my son. I figured healing would be the natural outcome of such prayers.

These verses became a song in the spring of 2020 with the release of *The Blessing.*[3] This song moves me to tears. We had the song performed during his memorial service and the verses embossed on a plaque that sits in his memorial garden.

I guess my prayers actually were answered. I have to believe my sweet Max is experiencing the blessing, grace, and peace in Heaven, I desperately prayed he would experience here on earth. I wish things had turned out differently so my precious boy would still be here with me, but I guess that's where faith plays a crucial role. I have to trust the Lord with the outcome. "I do believe; help me overcome my unbelief!" Mark 9:24b (NIV)

"I wish things had turned out differently...but I guess that's where faith plays a crucial role."

Nobody wants to be admitted to this club, but an immediate bond is formed when I meet someone else who is in it.

I recently read an article written by a mother who has lost a son.[4] A couple of things she wrote really resonated with me. First, she talks about the "club" of parents who have lost children. What an awful club it is! Nobody wants to be admitted to this club, but an immediate bond is formed when I meet someone who is in it. Only someone who has experienced the loss of a child can fully understand how it feels. How EVERYTHING is divided into two categories: before and after the loss.

Another point the author makes is that birthdays are particularly difficult. Not only do I have the memories of previous birthday celebrations and sadness over all the milestones Max will not achieve, but I also have physical pain as my body remembers giving birth to Max.

In the book, *The Body Keeps the Score*, author Bessel Van der Kolk.[5] suggests that our bodies remember, at a cellular level, all the trauma we've experienced in our lives. That's why on Max's birthday, my body, not just my mind, is remembering the day he was born. The physical sensations of pain and sorrow are rooted in this memory and will continue every year we celebrate his birthday without him.

When we lose a loved one, we can expect to grieve as long as we are breathing.

I just had another conversation where someone said, "You seem to be handling Max's passing well." That sentiment, as well as "You seem fine" is not accurate. Let me be clear, getting out of bed, going on with daily life, and occasionally smiling and laughing are not accurate indicators of being "fine." The pain, heartache, and desperation are always just below the surface. Since his passing, I have the recurring dream of going somewhere and seeing him there. Last night, I dreamt I went to the mall and ran into him. I said, "Oh my gosh, Lovey! I am so happy to see you. We thought we'd lost you!"

I recently heard that when we lose a loved one, we can expect to grieve as long as we are breathing. That sounds about right to me.

I know deep down God will continue to show up.

In the days following Max's death, a friend told us that we should be on the lookout for "God moments." She said God would show up in unexpected ways to comfort us and give us hope. I was conflicted. I thought, "I don't want comfort and hope. I want my son back."

I have to be honest; I haven't been on the lookout for God moments. However, as I look back on the last few months, I can see some.

One occurred a couple of weeks after his death. Max had a red Prius. He loved that little car partly because it got unbelievable gas mileage, but also because it represented independence to him. He lost his license after his epilepsy diagnosis in the summer of 2014, and that had been a big blow to his ego. He got it back briefly in the winter of 2017, but then he lost it again due to another seizure. Max's little red Prius represented a "come back" of sorts.

Just a few months before his death, Max took a dear friend for her driving test. She didn't have a vehicle of her own, so she asked him if she could take the test in his car. He was happy to oblige, and she passed. Although she didn't have a car, getting her license was an important step into adulthood and independence for her as well.

After Max's death, we knew he would want us to give his car to this friend, and she was thrilled! After signing over the title to her at the notary's office, we stood outside in the parking lot and prayed. Another customer from the office came charging out upon seeing us pray. Apparently, she had asked the Notary what we were doing, and the employee who had helped us told her. This customer was crying as she emerged from the office. She told us, "I just had to come out and join your prayer circle. I lost my son too, and my sister who is with me also lost her son. We know what you are going through, and we are so sorry. God will get you through this." Even I couldn't deny this God moment.

But I haven't been in the mood to look for God moments. In fact, I've been angry with God. I'm angry that my sweet son is gone. I'm angry Max did not experience his healing in this life. I'm angry he will not have the chance to get married, have children of his own, and make an impact in the world like I knew he could. I'm angry about all of Max's promise and potential gone to waste.

I know these feelings of anger will diminish over time. I hope that going forward, I can recognize God moments as they happen rather than just in retrospect. I know deep down God will continue to show up. I pray I can start to look for them.

"I haven't been in the mood to look for God moments... I've been angry with God. I'm angry that my sweet son is gone."

Max may have died but my love and my motherhood never will.

A few months after Max died, a friend sent me an article about what it means to be a bereaved mother.[6] It really struck me that the author's words could so profoundly describe what I am feeling.

She writes, "Losing my child affects me in so many ways: as a woman, a mother, a human being. It affects every aspect of me: spiritually, physically, mentally, and emotionally. There are days when I barely recognize myself in the mirror anymore."

Losing a child is not just emotional pain. It goes much deeper. Since we are physical, mental, emotional, and spiritual beings, it stands to reason the death of a child would deeply affect us in each of these areas.

I can totally relate to not recognizing myself in the mirror. Some days I look at my reflection and think, "How are you standing? How did you get out of bed? Why are you continuing on when you've lost something so beloved? Who are you?"

Most people have been sympathetic and compassionate. After all, it's only been a few months since we lost Max. However, every once in a while someone will try to "explain" our loss, or, even worse, they tell us about "the good" that will come out of it. I expect this will occur more frequently as time goes on, and people assume we have finished grieving.

Isn't it remarkable that someone might feel justified in telling me how I should or shouldn't be grieving? Even someone who has experienced the loss of a child has no right to do this. Grieving is an intensely personal experience. We all must find our way through it the best way we can. The grieving mother in the article goes on to say, "If I am to survive this, I must do what is best for me."

Notice she says, "If I survive this." Friends, do not assume it will be "when." Heck, even I shouldn't assume that I will survive this grief and loss. I will just try to take one day at a time, as cliché as that sounds. I will try to get out of bed each day and continue to pray for the strength and fortitude to carry this burden.

As the author so beautifully says, "My child may have died but my love – and my motherhood – never will." My Max may have died but my love and my motherhood never will.

Our sweet boy had the biggest heart.

In August of 2017, Bill and I renewed our wedding vows in the presence of our family and friends. We asked Max to give the toast. Due to his witty and sometimes snarky sense of humor, we were expecting a bit more of a "roast" than a toast. We could not have been more wrong. He shared the most beautiful tribute to Bill and me. He said, "...these things I know about love, I know from watching my parents for all these years. I have watched them share in each other's joys, work towards their relationship, and every day recommit themselves to each other. They are the best example of true love I know..." Our sweet boy had the biggest heart. He was an excellent writer, and I treasure these beautiful, affirming words we had the privilege to hear directly from him.

He was loving and deeply devoted to family. I often told him that one day he would make an excellent husband and father. He was skeptical but I knew his tenderness, compassion, and affection would allow him to love a wife and children well.

My sweet boy will not get that chance. I can't help but think we all missed out on this.

Lament is not a failure of faith, but an act of faith.

The sister of Sam's former roommate made us a graphic image of a family photo taken five years ago at the beach. It is a beautiful, creative reminder of a happy family vacation.

Since losing Max, we have been blown away by the kindness and thoughtfulness of countless people. In addition to our gratitude for friends, family, and in some cases, even strangers, we are still consumed by our deep sorrow and sadness. This paradox has led me to read about lament. I believe most people are not comfortable with lament, particularly those of us who call ourselves Christians. We feel like we need to get past our grief, find the meaning that often comes from trials, and emerge "better," not "bitter."

I found an article that rightfully points out that God can handle our pain, anger, and doubt, and lament is a constructive way to deal with these feelings, so they don't take on a destructive form. I'm taking comfort in this truth about lament: "Lament is not a failure of faith, but an act of faith. We cry out directly to God because deep down we know that our relationship with God counts; it counts to us, and it counts to God."[7]

I pray he is with Jesus in Heaven wearing a cute jacket and a sweet smile.

A cousin recently sent me a picture of a visit to her home more than twenty years ago. Max is sitting on top of a pony, while I stand alongside him in the photo. Both of us are smiling into the camera, happy to be together with family and experiencing the adventure of a pony ride.

The photo captures my sweet Max's beautiful, chubby, babyface. He was wearing my favorite jacket. It was reversible, plaid on one side and chambray on the other, and it had an elastic hood and cuffs. He wore it on walks in his stroller, and his little face and hands would get brown from the sun. He was my world, my pride, and my joy. I miss my baby boy so much! I pray he is with Jesus in Heaven wearing a cute jacket and a sweet smile.

"Blessed are those who mourn, for they will be comforted." MATTHEW 5:4 (NIV)

Do you know what's fun? Menopause and grief. Menopause is a new stage of life complete with hot flashes, weight gain, depression, insomnia, and intimacy challenges. Grief is also new and uncharted territory with some of the same symptoms.

Just as menopause can disrupt intimacy, so can grief. It is easy and tempting to be so inwardly focused that I forget about the people around me who still need my love and care.

When my perimenopausal night sweats started a couple of years ago, I began waking up between three and five times a night. Sometimes I would fall right back to sleep, while other times I would remain awake for hours. I remember thinking, "This lack of sleep is going to kill me." I have complained that I needed to spend ten to eleven hours in bed just to get seven to eight hours of sleep.

Combine night sweats with grieving, and it's a wonder I get any sleep at all. I wake up covered in sweat, and then my mind starts to race. Sometimes I wake up in the middle of a dream about Max, and I get so angry it's been interrupted. Some mornings I feel like I am physically, mentally, and emotionally one hundred years old.

I know the menopausal symptoms will eventually pass. However, I don't think my grief will ever end. Unfortunately, I expect grief to be my constant companion as long as I'm still walking on this earth. With God's grace, it will hopefully diminish, but I doubt it will ever leave me entirely. That is just the reality after losing a child. "Blessed are those who mourn, for they will be comforted." Matthew 5:4 (NIV)

"I should not assume God owed me healing for my son simply because I had prayed a certain prayer..."

While I most certainly play a part, my faith is by the grace and mercy of God.

When Max was about twelve, I was introduced to a more charismatic version of Christianity, by visiting a local church while on a mission trip to Costa Rica. For the first time, I was exposed to examples of the gifts of the Holy Spirit, such as speaking in tongues, being slain in the spirit, and faith healings.

Later, I remember a conversation about prayer with a friend who attended a local charismatic church. I told her I believed God desires us to pray for what we want and need, but ultimately I felt the best way to pray was how Jesus taught us, "Thy Will be Done." She thought this was a faulty prayer.

She explained that we must pray boldly and expectantly and not allow doubt to creep in, otherwise our prayers may not be answered. "Doubt indicates a lack of faith," she said.

In response, I remember using the example of a child's illness. I said, "If Max got sick, of course, I would pray for healing, but I would need to leave his healing in the hands of God." I told her I should not assume God owed me healing for my son simply because I had prayed a certain prayer or prayed in a particular way.

Those conversations occurred before Max got sick. Over the years, I have wondered if I tempted God through those conversations. Intellectually, I know that isn't the case. Sometimes though, I cannot shake the feeling that I brought on all of his health issues by my lack of faith.

Faith is a funny thing. We think it's all about us—how much we believe, when and how we acknowledge Jesus, and what we do as a result of our professed belief. Furthermore, we measure and compare it with the faith of others.

I think I am starting to realize that most things, faith included, are not all about me. My faith is not of my own volition. While I most certainly play a part, my faith is by the grace and mercy of God. I am thankful it doesn't all rest on my shoulders. I think God is able to deal with everything better than I am.

I could tell how he was feeling just by looking at his eyes.

Max was a colicky baby. Bill and I have joked that we actually invented the vibrating bouncy seat. We would put Max in his bouncy seat on top of the dryer and run it in order to soothe him when he cried. We also took many late-night car rides to lull him to sleep. If he wasn't eating or sleeping, he was crying. I fed him a lot.

At approximately four months, he outgrew the colic and became a sweet and mellow baby. He had a gorgeous round head that was too big for his body. We have several pictures where he looks like Humpty Dumpty.

My grandfather said he looked like "Spanky" from the television series, Little Rascals, filmed from 1938-1944. He also compared Max's large, dark brown, expressive eyes to black olives.

I loved those eyes. As he got older, people would say he had "sleepy" or "bedroom" eyes. They were beautiful and so expressive. I could tell how he was feeling just by looking at his eyes.

When his depression began I could see it in his eyes, and I could hardly stand it. I desperately wanted to take his pain away. I used to think, "Why can't it be me instead?" It would have been so much easier to handle, for me anyway.

The helplessness I felt over the years was profound. There were many times I felt hopeless as well. Now that the very worst has happened, I find myself feeling that way again. I don't want to wallow in hopelessness, but I'm not sure I know how NOT to wallow. It is just so unfair that we lost our precious boy.

Max was an early talker, and Mr. John dubbed him a "funny, verbal lollygagger."

When Max was about two years old, Bill taught him all the NFL football teams and their corresponding cities. Bill would say, "Pittsburgh," and Max would respond, "Steelers." Bill would say "Buffalo," and Max would say, "Bills." And so on. Needless to say, the guys in the neighborhood were impressed.

Max said the funniest things. One morning while I was getting ready for work, he left the house to go next door to ask our neighbor, Mr. John, to "open his banana." Great parenting on my part. Mr. John was the dad of Max's best friend, Joey. I'm pretty sure the banana stunt was just a ploy to play with Joey. Max was an early talker, and Mr. John dubbed him a "funny, verbal lollygagger."

One of my favorite memories of Max as a toddler was watching him watch the big kids in the neighborhood play kickball. He would stand on the sidewalk shouting, "Go, kids! Go, go, go, kids!"

Max continued to hone his communication skills in high school by joining the Speech and Debate team. I remember the team advisor telling us at a parent's meeting that the most successful debaters were those who stated their position with bold confidence whether it was true or not. I told Max that debate was an activity he was born for. He had strong opinions that he shared boldly, confidently, and freely. He got into many arguments with friends and family defending his position on various topics.

Unsurprisingly, he very quickly learned to outmaneuver me in an argument. I would say things like, "Because I said so" or "Because I'm the mother" when I couldn't refute him. More great parenting.

As difficult as he was to parent at times, I was so proud of his brilliance. I was so anxious to see what he would accomplish with that beautiful mind of his.

In his almost twenty-six years, he accomplished a lot. He wrote short stories, poetry, and songs. He created and published a magazine. He developed jokes for his stand-up comedy routines. He was a "verbal lollygagger" to the end. I miss talking with my sweet boy most of all.

Max was a protective, loving, and attentive big brother.

After they got over the annoying little brother/big brother phase, Max and Sam became great friends. Max would refer to Sam as "Max 2.0," an improved and updated version of himself.

One summer they went to a week-long camp in Michigan. Sam was eleven and Max was fourteen. Sam got terribly homesick and called us one evening begging us to come get him, which was about nine hours away. We promised to check on him in the morning hoping that he would feel better so we wouldn't have to make the drive. When we called the next morning, Sam agreed to stay another day because Max was with him. Max had left his group of friends to hang with his little brother.

Max was a protective, loving, and attentive big brother. He truly loved Sam. He wrote us a note before he passed, and in it he said, "Sam, I love you and I'm sorry if I was never able to express how proud I am to be your brother." Theirs was a relationship of mutual love and respect.

Shortly after Max passed, Sam said he didn't know who he was going to talk to now about life's big issues. They were a good pair. Max could pontificate, and Sam was a patient listener.

It breaks my heart that Sam lost his big brother and best friend. We all feel Max's absence deeply.

My sweet boy inspired love and admiration.

In the summer of 2018, Max moved into a house in the city. It was on a quiet, residential street of well-maintained homes. On either side of him and across the street lived beautiful, elderly, Black women. I referred to them as Max's Black grandmas.

These lovely ladies looked out for and doted on my sweet boy. They brought him meals, gave him advice, and tried to keep him in line. When Max was planning a party, he would go knock on their doors to tell them in advance.

If I ran into them while visiting Max, they would tell me what a "nice young man" he was. One time the grandma across the street told me she had seen him smoking on the roof of his front porch. She told me, "I came out and shouted for him to get down before he fell and hurt himself."

These ladies came to the funeral home visitation even though it was far from their homes. They got lost on the way but persevered in order to pay their respects. One of them told me, "He never disrespected me" and this was high praise indeed. These ladies making the effort to attend his visitation was one of the kindest gestures following his death. My sweet boy inspired love and admiration. I am so proud of him.

A Celebration of Life in Photos

July-October

Max & Sam

He truly loved Sam... he wrote us a note before he passed and in it he said, "Sam, I love you and I'm sorry if I was never able to express how proud I am to be your brother."

Our renewal of vows: Max said, "...these things I know about love, I know from watching my parents for all these years..."

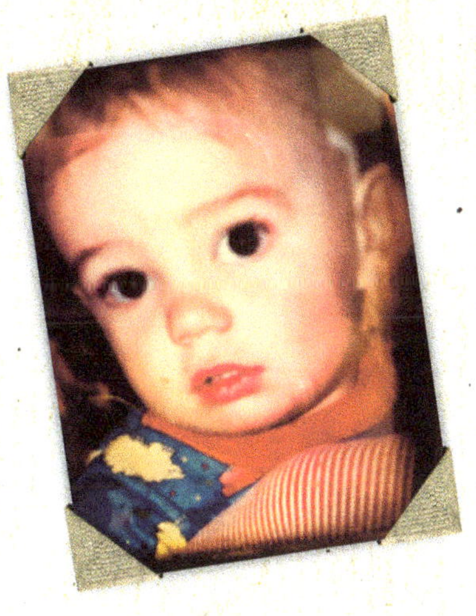

Baby Max
beautiful, big, brown eyes

"funny, verbal lollygagger."

I pray he is with Jesus in Heaven
wearing a cute jacket and a sweet smile.

the Beach Graphic

NOVEMBER & DECEMBER

I miss my sweet boy so much sometimes it's hard to breathe.

As I was contemplating our first Thanksgiving without our sweet Max, a picture from a previous Thanksgiving came up on Facebook. He had gained weight from all his meds and was not feeling particularly good about himself. Regardless, he had begun doing stand-up comedy at local venues. Seriously, who has the guts and talent to do such a thing?!

He was the most interesting person. He was tremendously resilient until he wasn't. I miss my sweet boy so much sometimes it's hard to breathe. His absence during the holiday season seems to enlarge the hole in my heart.

2020 has been a difficult year for all, and everyone's holidays will look different. If you're fortunate enough to have your beautiful children with you, hold them close and cherish the memories you'll be making. Every memory is a gift.

"You are braver than you believe, stronger than you seem, and smarter than you think."

During the years I was praying for Max, I had many conversations with others about his struggles. Friends and acquaintances would say, "He's going to have a tremendous testimony once he comes through all of this." I agreed. As a little boy, he was deeply spiritual. He had an unusual interest in God and a profound understanding of faith. I remember his response to the question, "What's the difference between happiness and joy?" He said, "Happiness is due to circumstance, but joy comes from the Lord." What a concept for a little boy to grasp!

Since he passed, I have had numerous conversations with people about "where to go from here." Recently a friend said to me, "I just know you will have an impact on many people due to your experience. You will have a tremendous testimony." But I don't want a tremendous testimony. That's what I wanted for my Max.

He was the writer. I thought he could write a book about overcoming obstacles, about coming through a crisis of faith, about seeing the Lord perform miracles. Now he doesn't have that chance.

One of my deepest desires is to honor my precious son in his death. I guess that is why I am recording these reflections. I hope to help other parents who have lost a child, particularly to suicide, help people better understand how someone who has lost a child feels, and help everyone, including myself, better accept a loved one who lives with mental illness.

I used to tell Max, "Your depression doesn't define you. It's not who you are." I didn't want him to feel like he was a victim of his illness. Many people learn to live with depression through a combination of medication, therapy, self-care, and strong support systems. I knew he had the support and grit to overcome the challenges of his illnesses, but he didn't feel that way. I saw qualities in him that he did not see in himself.

continued on next page

As a small boy, he had a Winnie the Pooh teddy bear. He loved Winnie the Pooh! He slept with him and dragged him around everywhere. We watched Winnie the Pooh videos and read Winnie the Pooh books. I have always loved the Christopher Robin quote to Winnie the Pooh, "You are braver than you believe, stronger than you seem, and smarter than you think."(A. A. Milne). Just like Pooh, my boy was all these things. He just didn't know it.

Jesus Saves.

During one of Max's depressive episodes, we had a frank conversation about faith. He told Bill and me, "I don't believe in God anymore. If God exists, He wouldn't have given me all these problems." Our son had lost his faith. We could understand why because we may have felt the same in his shoes.

About a year later, he started to sketch. He made meaningful drawings for Bill, Sam, and me. The one he drew for me was of Jesus. It was a sketch of Jesus' face with the words, "Jesus saves." It was beautiful! Not only did I love it because my talented boy sketched it for me, but it gave me hope that Max would return to his faith. It gave me hope that Max's faith was still inside him. Yes, it was buried beneath bitterness, skepticism, cynicism, and more, but I believe it was still inside him, nonetheless.

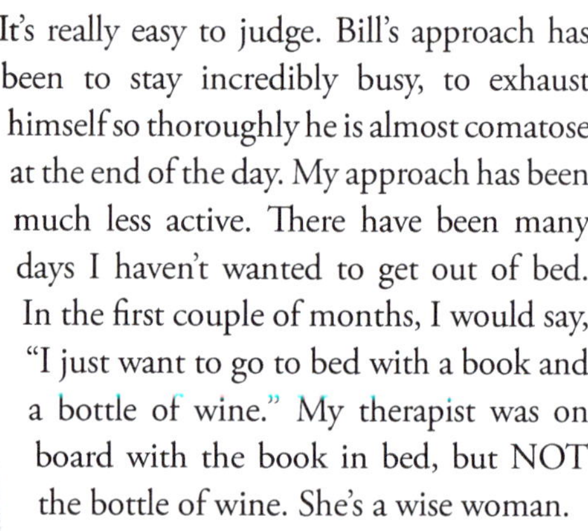

His faith was such an important part of his early years, and our church played a critical role in helping Max explore and deepen his faith. Our pastors assured us throughout his life and since his death, that Max may have wandered from Jesus, but Jesus never wandered from Max. That truth has been incredibly comforting.

That sketch has continued to be a beacon of hope for me. It hangs in my office. We printed it on the program for Max's memorial service. My sister-in-law had it printed on t-shirts she sold to benefit the American Foundation for Suicide Prevention.

I am incredibly thankful for this present from my son. It is a visual reminder of his creativity and giftedness. Every time I look at the sketch, I am assured that Max is in the loving arms of Jesus and that Max is finally healed and whole. As Max told me in his sketch, "Jesus Saves."

"You and Bill will make it through this, but only if you don't judge each other for the way you grieve."

There are some estimates that approximately 80% of couples will divorce following the death of a child. Those statistics are abysmal.[8] I understand how it could happen. Bill and I are handling Max's loss so differently. Shortly after he passed, my therapist told me, "You and Bill will make it through this, but only if you don't judge each other for the way you grieve." I am so grateful for her wise words.

It's really easy to judge. Bill's approach has been to stay incredibly busy, to exhaust himself so thoroughly he is almost comatose at the end of the day. My approach has been much less active. There have been many days I haven't wanted to get out of bed. In the first couple of months, I would say, "I just want to go to bed with a book and a bottle of wine." My therapist was on board with the book in bed, but NOT the bottle of wine. She's a wise woman.

Sometimes when Bill is in a manic state, I feel pressure to get up and get moving. Sometimes this makes me feel better, and sometimes it just makes me resentful.

I am so very thankful for therapy. Bill and I were both established with therapists before Max passed. We had also been seeing a marriage counselor. Thank God we had these resources in place. The last six months would have been much more difficult otherwise.

I have to believe that he's finally whole and healed.

Shortly after Max passed, a cousin gave me a picture of him with her two children. Max loved those kids. He used to call them "genius babies" because they were so smart. The picture was taken when they came to visit us in Pittsburgh for their spring break. We met Max for lunch in the city before going to the Science Center. It was a cold and gray March day.

I remember Max was struggling. It's hard to get through a long, gray, Pittsburgh winter, and it had taken a toll on his mental health. He was also in a toxic relationship that would end badly several months later. When I look at that picture, I can see the pain and weariness on his handsome face. He had the most beautifully expressive brown eyes, and I can see his struggles reflected in them.

Max had many people who loved him. He had a strong support system of family and friends, but it just wasn't enough. It makes me so sad to admit this. I guess part of being a mom is thinking we can love our kids through anything. We like to think we have more control than we actually do.

"I have to believe that he's in a better place...that my sweet son is with the Lord."

I recently heard a well-known pastor say that he fully surrendered his children to God when they were young. I thought, "How in the world does someone do that?"

I tried to fully surrender Max over to God, but then I would gradually pull him back because I so desperately wanted to make him better. Sure, I prayed that God would heal him, but when that prayer continued to go unanswered, I thought, "I guess it's up to me."

I have to believe he's in a better place. I have to believe that my sweet son is with the Lord. I have to believe that he's finally whole and healed. I have to believe these things. My hope and faith rest in them.

He really was the most interesting person.

I have often said Max was the most interesting person I knew. He had many gifts and talents, but one of his great passions was music. He formed a band, called 'The Young Giants,' while in high school, and he continued to form bands with friends in the subsequent years. He had a mini recording studio set up in his house. He was passionate about discovering and making music.

He loved all types of music, including punk, hardcore, alternative, rock, hip hop, rap, and country. He had recently talked about writing a book or blog on the hardcore punk rock scene in the US. He was something of an expert, and he would have done a great job at recounting the history of this unique genre he so loved.

continued on next page

A couple of months before he passed, he recorded two country music radio shows and aired them on social media. He called them Hardcore Country, and his motivation was to convince everyone of the merits of country music. During these two shows, he played classic country and new, cutting-edge country songs. His on-air commentary was classic Max: funny, snarky, blunt, and a bit profane. I hadn't heard most of the music before, but I became a convert.

I like listening to country music now as a nod to Max and his eclectic taste. I think it's unusual for a person to have such broad taste in music, but I suspect each genre fulfilled a different need in him. Each genre gave a voice to something he felt, which is why music so deeply resonated with him. He really was the most interesting person.

I may wander from Jesus,
but Jesus will never wander from me.

My faith has been badly shaken by Max's death. I feel like all those years of prayers were futile, and my many tears were for naught. I've been angry at God for not healing my son, and ultimately for taking him.

Curiously, my daily habit of bible reading and devotions has continued. I may not have the same level of desire, but I have continued, nonetheless. I've heard that's why daily quiet time with the Lord is important so that when troubles and trials come the habit will already be in place. That's been true for me.

Having said that, my prayer life has been pretty pathetic over the last six months. It's been hard for me to pray due to my anger, my sadness, my hopelessness, and my despair. One of the greatest gifts has been the prayers of others. We know there are literally dozens of people who are praying for us. Countless other people have prayed WITH us, and that has truly made a difference.

We are blessed with a caring community—friends, and acquaintances who continue to send cards, notes, and other reminders of their thoughts and prayers. We have a friend who has sent us a bible verse almost every day for the last six months.

I hope I will be able to pray again as I did in the past. I hope the distance I feel from God will diminish over time. I should tell myself what our pastors told us about Jesus and Max all those years. I may wander from Jesus, but Jesus will never wander from me.

It has made me wonder not what was wrong with
his heart that allowed him to feel things so deeply,
but what's wrong with mine that I don't.

Max was an incredibly sensitive child. As a baby, he cried when I played lullabies. He seemed to be deeply affected by sad songs or sad movies.

When he was about four years old, his favorite movie was *The Lion King*.[9] He watched it countless times. During one sad and tense scene, he would stand up, back out of the room, and could be heard shouting, "Run Simba, Run!"

He also loved other movies as a child but would cry every time he watched a sad scene. My sweet boy had a tender and sensitive heart.

As he got older his heart remained tender, but he learned how to wrap it in sarcasm and cynicism. He was witty and funny, but his humor would also cut at times. He was deeply affected by what was happening in the world. He once took a young mother into the store to buy diapers, only to watch her walk back into the store to return them and collect the money.

You might expect that an experience like this would have left him jaded, but it didn't. He kept trying to help and speak up for others. He seemed to allow all the negativity in the world to seep into his heart and mind. He didn't seem to be able to filter it. It has made me wonder not what was wrong with his heart that allowed him to feel things so deeply, but what's wrong with mine that I don't.

I used to fantasize about running away, and sometimes I still do.

A few years into Max's health issues, my parents' health began to decline. Both my mom and dad suffer from deteriorating neurological conditions, and it has been difficult to watch their conditions worsen.

Dealing with an unwell child is difficult, but dealing with both an unwell child and failing, elderly parents is even worse. Max fretted and worried about them, while they fretted and worried about him. I fretted and worried about all three of them! There were times the stress of it all really got to me. I used to fantasize about running away, and sometimes I still do.

My mom has taken Max's death very hard. He was her first grandchild, and she babysat him when I returned to work after his birth. They had a special bond.

Due to my dad's dementia diagnosis, we chose not to tell him about Max's death. The health care workers in the Memory Care unit where he resides advised against it. It's been incredibly hard to have my dad ask how Max is doing. Recently he's stopped asking about Max, most likely due to his worsening dementia, but I am thankful. It was just too difficult to smile and say, "Max is fine, Dad."

While I didn't expect my parents to get better, I really expected that Max would. He had been seizure-free for more than two years prior to his death. He was seeing a therapist he really liked, and he had a beautiful girlfriend whom he loved dearly. He seemed to finally understand the connection between nutrition, exercise, and mental health. We were hopeful that his depression medications would start to work better in conjunction with a healthier lifestyle. Such was not the case.

The COVID pandemic hit, he lost his job, his gym closed, isolation set in, the election mudslinging worsened, and the social and racial unrest escalated. It was all too much for him to take. He left a note that said he felt like he was in a burning building, and the only thing he could do was jump.

It's tragic and painful that he felt death was his only option. The fact that he's gone is heart-rending and his loss has impacted us far more deeply than we could have anticipated. Although we haven't experienced peace since his death, I am thankful he is finally at peace.

As we faced our first holidays without Max, we decided to spend the month of November in Florida. We are fortunate to have a second home in Naples, Florida, and it is a respite. Although we couldn't justify spending Christmas away from family, we decided that Thanksgiving would be better spent elsewhere. Sam visited for the holiday, as well as some dear friends. It was a nice alternative to a holiday spent at home filled with memories of Max.

…a calm refuge in the midst of a storm, a respite for my heavy heart.

As I sit here on our last morning in Florida, I'm struck by how restorative the sun and warmth can be. It is cooler this morning than normal, but of course, the sun is shining. This is my happy place.

My parents used to spend the winters in Florida, and every spring break for about fifteen years we visited them with Max and Sam. I have happy memories of time spent on the beach and at the pool with loving grandparents. I think Max would say this was a happy place for him as well.

He was supposed to visit us here in Florida twice in the last year, but both trips were canceled. Although I was disappointed at the time, perhaps it was for the best considering what's happened. This place remains a calm refuge in the midst of a storm, a respite for my heavy heart. It's been a way to press pause on my grief because this home is not full of memories of Max like his childhood home in Pittsburgh.

I'm thankful for this place, so very thankful for sunshine, warmth, palm trees, sunsets, simplicity, new friends, and new memories.

It's like trying to go on living without an arm, or a leg, or a heart.

Since losing Max, my recurring thought has been, "I just want to be with my boy." It is not that I love him more than Bill and Sam; it's just that I miss him so much it feels like a part of me is missing. It's like trying to go on living without an arm, or a leg, or a heart. How do I do it?

"I miss him so much, it feels like a part of me is missing."

My desire to be present for Bill and Sam is one motivation for me. I need to get out of bed for them. I need to shower and dress for them. I need to get through the day for them.

As Christmas approaches, I have no Christmas spirit. I have no desire to decorate or celebrate. I keep putting off getting a Christmas tree. I will eventually do all those things not because I want to, but because I feel like I have to. Sam is still here, and he deserves a Christmas. He deserves a mom who is present and involved. I just wish I felt more motivated to do the things I normally love to do this time of year.

Max loved the holidays. He loved getting together with family and friends. He enjoyed picking out gifts for the people he loved, and he was a generous and thoughtful gift giver. On Christmas morning, the four of us would sit around the fire and take turns opening presents. I don't know how we will do it this year. His chair, his stocking, and his seat at the dinner table will be glaringly empty. He always sat at the head of the table opposite Bill, his honor as the firstborn. How will we possibly celebrate without him this year?

I must face the fact that we will always have to celebrate these events without him now.

I know there will be a million heartbreaks this Christmas. One was delivered yesterday. Every year Max and Sam would get a Christmas card and check from Pop-pop Ed, their step-grandfather on Bill's side. Bill's mom died back in 1998. We're pretty sure she extracted a deathbed wish from him to faithfully send Christmas gifts in her absence. We have not seen Ed in years, but every December a card arrives.

He always included one check made out to both Max and Sam. When they were little it wasn't a problem, as I would simply deposit the check and give cash to each one. Since they have gotten older it's become a bit more complicated. The card would typically arrive while Sam was still away at college, and Max was living on his own in the city. Sometimes one would sign it over to the other and deposit it. Sometimes they would go to the bank together to cash it. Sometimes one or the other would try a mobile deposit, which may or may not work. It was kind of like a Christmas puzzle to be solved.

Yesterday the card arrived from Pop-pop Ed. As usual, it contained only one check, but this year it was made out to Sam. Only Sam. No Max. It felt like a knife through my heart. It may sound strange, but this was so surprising it took my breath away. I SHOULDN'T have been surprised. I KNOW Max is gone, but things like this make it seem so final, so permanent.

People ask what it's been like for us on his birthday and Thanksgiving. I dreaded those days as they approached, but then I was gratefully surprised to enjoy some portions of both days. Oddly, it's the day after that's been the toughest for me. Although this is our year of firsts (first birthday, first Thanksgiving, and first Christmas without him), I must face the fact that we will always have to celebrate these events without him now. Maybe that's why the days *after* a holiday are so awful for me.

It's customary in the US to say, "Merry Christmas!" and in the UK they say, "Happy Christmas!" There will be nothing "merry" or "happy" about our Christmas this year. Perhaps I will coin a new phrase, "Miserable Christmas." Think it'll catch on?

Max will never get engaged. Max will never have a baby. Max will never turn twenty-six.

When Max and Sam were eight and five respectively, we attended a Christmas party at a local school for urban youth. Our church had partnered with the school to provide Christmas gifts for their students. We all gathered on an early December day to share a meal and give the children their gifts.

At the party, we met a darling little boy, Rafael. He was eight years old and he had beautiful, soulful, brown eyes, just like Max. Have I mentioned I am partial to brown eyes?

As the children were called to receive a gift, Rafael's name was not called. At the end of the event, every child in attendance had received a gift except him. He was heartbroken, and so was I.

continued on next page

I made it my mission to purchase a gift for him the following week and deliver it to the school. I don't really remember how it happened, but somehow his mom got in touch to thank me. A friendship was born.

At first, we started to take Rafael along on family outings to the zoo, Science Center, or Children's Museum. Then we periodically invited him to spend weekends with us. Later we got to know his whole family and began to celebrate Christmas with them every year. It has become an annual highlight for both of our families.

Rafael recently got engaged, had a baby, and celebrated his twenty-sixth birthday. It was bittersweet. We are so happy for him and so proud of the beautiful man he's become. Rafael is like another son to us, AND he has been able to do things Max won't be able to do. Max will never get engaged. Max will never have a baby. Max will never turn twenty-six. It's just so hard!

We are so thankful for Rafael and his beautiful new family. We love them deeply. We just wish Rafael's new baby could have grown up with Max's children the same way Max and Rafael grew up together.

We loved his unique way of seeing the world.

We decorated the Christmas tree, and it was as painful as I anticipated. We have many handmade ornaments the boys made in school or that others gave to us in recognition of milestones. We have the "Baby's First Christmas" ornaments and personalized family ornaments that list all of our names. We even have one commemorating Max's high school band, The Young Giants.

The most difficult for us to unwrap and hold were the ones Max made himself. They are precious. Max and Sam attended the same preschool and elementary schools, so we tend to have duplicates. Max made an ornament one year, and Sam would make the same ornament a few years later. Their finished products truly reflect their personalities. Sam's ornaments are neat and orderly and look very similar to the teacher's example. Max's ornaments are another story. He took creative license and created a more unique version. Last year, as we were decorating the tree together, Max said jokingly, "Was something wrong with me? Why are my ornaments so weird?" We all laughed.

Max marched to the beat of his own drum. We loved his unique way of seeing the world. My special boy never fit into a box. We miss him so much it hurts.

Platitudes minimize my loss and my feelings.

During the years of dealing with Max's illnesses, several well-intentioned people said to me, "God won't give you more than you can handle." I hated hearing that platitude because it's simply not true. The bible is full of stories of people who were given more than they could handle. Elijah prayed he would die (1 Kings 19). Jesus prayed for His cup of suffering to be taken away (Matthew 26).

In our broken world, we all have more than we can "handle." I know our family did. How is anyone expected to "handle" the serious illness and subsequent death of a child? How was Max supposed to "handle" his depression and epilepsy?

> *"In our broken world, we all have more than we can handle."*

Other platitudes like, "Let Go and Let God," "When God closes one door, another one opens," or "Where God guides, God provides" all set my teeth on edge. How do I possibly "let go" of

"The terminology around mental illness is inadequate."

Max? How is it possible to view Max's passing as an opportunity for another "open door?' How can I reconcile the loss of a beloved child with "God's guidance?" These platitudes minimize my loss and my feelings, and I don't believe that's what God desires.

Christian platitudes like these contain erroneous theology and need to be eliminated as a response to those who are suffering. They are hurtful and dismissive and not comforting or helpful at all! May we offer more compassion to each other and lean on the One who can help us handle whatever comes our way. His name is Jesus.

This world is broken, and we all have to deal with more than we can handle. It's a question of how we handle it. Will we become better or bitter? I would like to become better, but I totally understand how the root of bitterness can grow in one's heart and mind. Life is unfair. Having a child who suffered as Max did is unfair. Having to deal with his death is unfair.

Photos are great, but videos reveal his essence.

As a child and teen, Max was actively involved at church. When he was in eighth grade, he began to serve as a teen leader in our middle school youth ministry. He and a group of other teens planned games and activities for the weekly meetings.

We have a video of Max from his days serving in that ministry. It was filmed as a way for the middle school students to get to know their ministry leaders. Each teen leader was interviewed and was asked to share some personal information about themselves.

It's classic Max. He introduced himself as "Maxwell Aquarius Blechman" (his middle name is Alexander). He declared his favorite color to be "monochrome" due to his color-blindness. He stated his superpower was the ability to eat a giant salad in "thirteen seconds flat." He claimed to be commissioned by the "World Salad Eating Commission" as the Best Salad Eater in America.

What a quirky sense of humor! I am so thankful to be able to listen to his voice and watch his mannerisms on videos like these. Photos are great, but the videos reveal his personality, his essence. They help when I am missing my sweet boy.

Depression is so misunderstood.

The terminology around mental illness is inadequate, and it frustrates me. The word "depressed" is used to describe everything from simply feeling blue to the much more severe clinical depression or major depressive disorder. I think this is one reason why depression is so misunderstood. During the years that Max was ill, we heard all kinds of comments about his depression.

"What does he have to be depressed about?"
"Has he prayed about it?"
"Why doesn't he just feel better?"

continued on next page

"I don't believe in depression."
"I get depressed too. He just needs to pull himself out of it."

The misconceptions are vast. Bill and I also held misconceptions early on in Max's illness, and there was much we didn't understand. I tried to educate myself, but much of what I learned frightened me, and I was tempted to put my head in the sand.

I remember, shortly after his diagnosis, I went to a NAMI (National Alliance on Mental Illness) support group. It was a group for the family members of those living with a mental illness. With each person's story, it became more and more difficult for me to listen. I never went back.

I wish now that I had done a better job of learning more about what it was like for Max to live with a mental illness. I was so focused on his healing that I believe I lacked the compassion and empathy he needed in the moment. I wasn't comfortable just being present with him and offering him comfort. I will always regret this.

Sometimes mental anguish is so great, it demands an outlet.

I have started biting my nails again. It was a habit I had as a child, but I stopped years ago. Since Max passed, I have been picking and biting them so much they throb. In some ways, it's a distraction. My emotional pain is so intense, it's kind of a relief to have physical pain to focus on instead. I know that might sound weird to those who haven't experienced acute emotional pain and loss. I never understood cutting or other forms of self-harm before, but I do now.

Max used to talk about self-sabotage or self-harm—it scared me. I would say, "Just don't do it!" I now understand it's not that simple. Sometimes mental anguish is so great, it demands an outlet.

It breaks my heart that it took his death to help me understand some of what he experienced. Since he passed, I now understand what it's like to lack the motivation to get out of bed. I now understand what it's like to be apathetic towards life. I now understand what it's like not to care whether I live or die.

I hope these feelings pass, but in the meantime, they help me understand my sweet boy better. I am relieved he's not suffering anymore. Rest in peace, my love.

Finding a medication to treat depression was like trying on shoes without knowing your size.

Over the years, Max tried several different medications to help manage his depression and anxiety. Unfortunately, many antidepressants lower a person's seizure threshold, so it was tricky to find a balance between helping his depression and not making his epilepsy worse.

A doctor once told him that finding a medication to treat depression was like trying on shoes without knowing your size. How discouraging! There is still so much we don't know about the brain. It's a complex organ. Much more research is necessary to better understand how to successfully treat brain-related illnesses, like depression, anxiety, and epilepsy.

Max was incredibly intelligent, but his brain was often his greatest gift AND his biggest curse. I desperately wish God had answered our prayers for his healing in this world.

"His brain was his greatest gift and his biggest curse."

Compassion is so critical when trying to support a loved one who is living with a mental illness.

Words are powerful, particularly the words of a parent. Our words carry tremendous weight with our children. We have the ability to build up or tear down, depending on what we say.

"We have the ability to build up or tear down..."

When I think of some of the things I said to Max over the years, it makes me want to cry. I didn't understand. I was confused. I was afraid. I was consumed by gut-wrenching worry. As a result, I said some hurtful things.

During one of his hospital stays for suicide ideation, I said to him, "You're killing me." He was depressed and suicidal, and I told him that he was killing me!

I will regret those words and others until the day I die. Compassion is so critical when trying to support a loved one who is living with a mental illness. Sometimes we mistakenly believe that they have a choice in how they are feeling, and/or that it's their choice to be ill. Why do we treat mental illness so differently than physical illness? If Max had developed diabetes, I know I would not have responded in the same way.

We must change the narrative about mental illness if we are to truly support and encourage those who are living with it. Help me do this. Please.

He used his voice and his privilege to call out injustice when he saw it, and I am very proud of his courage and integrity.

Shortly before Max died by suicide, George Floyd was murdered. Max attended a protest in Pittsburgh to offer his support against police brutality. He was deeply disturbed by the racial injustice and division over it in our country. He was deeply committed to fighting for equality and fairness.

Max met a friend at the protest who was there taking photos. The police ended up using teargas to break up the crowd. Max was in the middle of a crowd when a can of teargas landed at his feet. He picked it up and threw it back towards the police officers. His friend snapped a photo just after the canister left his hand. It's a remarkable photo. Max's friend sent it to us just after his death.

When I look at this picture, I see a man taking a stand against wrongs being committed. I see a person who was deeply impacted by the unjust and unfair treatment of Black people. I see my beloved son who was struggling.

After the protest, Max became paranoid. He was convinced the police would be looking for him. He was afraid he would be arrested. His mental state continued to deteriorate.

I can't accurately describe how proud I am to be his mom. He was an advocate for those who could not or would not stand up for themselves. He used his voice and his privilege to call out injustice when he saw it, and I am very proud of his courage and integrity.

Being a parent is like having your heart walk around outside of your body.

I just finished the book, *Fear Gone Wild,* by Kayla Stoecklein.[10] In it she describes her husband's battle with mental illness and his ultimate death by suicide. It's an honest and heartbreaking portrayal of what they experienced. Much of the book resonated with me. Stoecklein wrote about grief being a consequence of love. How true! When we love someone, we open ourselves up to hurt and grief.

"Grief is a consequence of love."

I've heard it said that being a parent is like having your heart walk around outside of your body. Our hearts are exposed, and our children's hurts become our hurts. Their pain becomes our pain. This was so true with Max. I was deeply affected by his highs and his lows, and his pain became my pain.

You've probably heard the phrase, "You are only as happy as your most unhappy child." A therapist told me I could NOT live by this mantra, yet I honestly didn't know how not to. Sure, I had times of happiness during the years Max was struggling, but his struggles were never completely out of my mind. Worry for him was my constant companion. And now my sorrow over losing him is.

Life is hard. Christmas will stink. Friends are priceless.

A friend came to visit me this past week. She lost her husband last Christmas, and her two teenage sons lost their dad and best friend.

It's so validating to talk with her. She's not pretending everything is okay. In fact, she was completely honest about what she and her boys are going through. Our families have been friends for years. Although her boys are about ten years younger than Max and Sam, they were buddies. We spent many summer days out on the lake with our boats tied together, swimming, tubing, and wakeboarding with them. Looking back, our lives sure seemed picture-perfect.

I said to her, "Thank goodness neither of us knew what was coming. I don't think we could have handled it." I believe this is one of God's greatest mercies. If we knew what our futures held, we would be paralyzed with dread and fear. We wouldn't be able to live every day to the fullest. Or maybe it's just me who feels this way. I don't think I'm a pessimist, but perhaps this is the litmus test.

The last thing I said to her was, "Life is hard. Christmas will stink. Friends are priceless." It sounds like a country song. Max would be proud.

"If we knew what our futures held, we would be paralyzed with dread and fear. We wouldn't be able to live every day to the fullest."

That's tension of parenting, isn't it?
Understanding how and when to let go.

When Max was experiencing a depressive episode, he would almost always isolate himself, reportedly a common response in people living with depression. I would say to him, "Get up. Go outside. Call a friend. Do something." Like so many other things since his death, I understand the urge to isolate better now.

There are days I don't want to leave my room, don't want to see anyone, and don't want to do anything. It's ironic, but the very things which may help a person feel better when depressed are the things they're reluctant or unable to do. I know that firsthand now.

I have friends who will not allow me to isolate for long. They call, text, or drop by. They suggest walks, coffee dates, shopping or other activities to keep me engaged. Sometimes it's exhausting, but overall, I am thankful for their care and concern.

It also makes me wonder if I should have done more with Max. It makes me think about the line between support and interference. While he was alive, I tried to show him my support by verbalizing my confidence in him. I didn't want to send him the message that somehow I didn't think he could manage on his own. He already felt inadequate and insecure. I really focused on telling him, "You got this!"

Looking back, I don't know if this was the right approach. If I had done things differently, would they have turned out differently? These are the questions and regrets that keep me up at night. I try to tell myself I did the best I could. I fiercely loved Max, and I tried my best to encourage and support him.

"I did the best I could."

As strange as it may sound, I am glad he was a young adult and not a young child when he became ill. If he had been younger when it all started, I'm sure I would have become obsessed with his health issues and would have ruined his life and mine, smothering and stifling him.

As it was, he was nineteen when he got his diagnosis. He wanted to manage his health on his own, albeit sometimes poorly. I was both proud of his independence and sick over my lack of control. I was encouraged by his autonomy and constantly anxious about how he was handling his health. That's the tension of parenting, isn't it? Understanding how and when to let go. I just keep telling myself I did the best I could with what I had and with what I knew at the time. I hope my sweet Max would say the same.

Life is messy. I am in the middle of messy.

I continue to hear that the opposite of faith is fear. Not unbelief, but fear. Does this mean faith and fear cannot coexist? Does it mean fear indicates a lack of faith? I don't believe so.

"Fear not" is in the bible 365 times, which is one for every day of the year. God knew we needed this reminder. Life can be beautiful and terrible. Life can be full of joy and full of pain.

It's not an "either/or," it's an "and/both." We can be people of faith and still have serious bouts of fear.

"We can be people of faith and still have serious bouts of fear."

We want to wrap things up so neatly, especially tragic things. I think this is particularly true for believers. We want to focus on the victorious end rather than the messy middle. Well, life is messy. I am in the middle of "messy." Please don't discount my messiness. I am hopeful God will bring "beauty from the ashes," (Isaiah 61:3) but right now I am sitting in ashes. Don't try to sweep them up, just sit with me. I believe Jesus is sitting with me, quietly and sweetly. You can too.

I believe God will wait patiently for me.

Over the years when we would receive a crisis call from Max, Bill and I would respond very differently. I would get sad, and Bill would get mad. Not mad at Max, but blindingly angry at the issues our sweet boy was facing. I would simply cry.

One point of contention between Bill and me was prayer. I know that sounds strange. I would want to pray, and Bill would be so angry and frustrated he simply could not. I don't want to make it sound like I am more spiritual, that my faith is somehow stronger and bigger. I just felt so helpless and hopeless in those moments that prayer was the only thing I knew to do.

"It's hard for me to pray. It's hard to even know how to pray."

Since Max passed, my prayer life has suffered. It's hard for me to pray. It's hard to even know how to pray. I think God is okay with this. There are lots of other people praying for us, for me. I am hopeful the day will come when prayer once again becomes the only thing I know to do. In the meantime, I believe God will wait patiently for me. I'm thankful for His grace.

What we do not understand, we come to fear, and what we fear, we come to hate.

I am reading a fantastical fiction book about magical children called *The House in the Cerulean Sea.*[11] I read a paragraph that deeply resonated with me. It basically says what we do not understand, we come to fear, and what we fear, we come to hate.

I see this played out all around me in politics, relationships, and life as a whole. It resonated with me because I felt that way about Max's depression.

I am embarrassed to admit it, but I could never fully understand the dynamics of his mental illness. I couldn't understand how someone with so much potential and promise was unable to see it in himself. I didn't understand why he couldn't do all the things seemingly within his control to help himself feel better. I attempted to educate myself about depression and anxiety; I learned many discouraging and disheartening things. I couldn't wrap my mind around it, and I just wanted it to go away.

My lack of understanding led to fear, and over time my fear became hatred. I wasn't aware of it at the time, but I had come to see his illness as an evil force holding him back and holding him down instead of a complex medical condition that required patience and acceptance from me. I didn't have to fully understand it, I just needed to accept it as a result of living in this world.

"My lack of understanding led to fear, and over time my fear became hatred."

I am so sorry to have had this realization after Max passed. Imagine the validation he would have felt if I had stopped struggling against it and accepted it for what it was. He suffered from a disease. He did not choose it. He certainly didn't want it. I am sure my convoluted feelings about his illnesses were obvious to him, and I cannot help thinking he felt judged and misunderstood. I am so sorry, my love. I hope you can forgive me.

"It's tough to accept unanswered prayers...even harder to accept an outcome so drastically different than the one you want."

I prayed. I begged. I pleaded.

The 'Serenity Prayer,' written by Reinhold Niebuhr, starts with, "God, grant me the serenity to accept the things I cannot change, the courage to change the things I can, and the wisdom to know the difference." This prayer hangs beside my bed, and I memorized it several years ago.

Most people are only familiar with this first line, but it is actually much longer and more beautiful in its entirety. It goes on to suggest that we "accept this sinful world as it is and not as I would have it." While this is very convicting, it is also tremendously difficult to live out. There is so much pain and brokenness in the world, much of it I do not want to accept and would like to change.

When Max got sick, I desperately wanted things to be different. I fought tooth and nail against his diagnoses. I didn't want to accept them because to accept them felt like defeat. I prayed. I begged. I pleaded. It's tough to accept unanswered prayers. It is even harder to accept an outcome so drastically different than the one you want. I'm still trying to figure out how to accept his passing. I'm not sure I ever will.

I am heartbroken over all the lost opportunities.

We celebrated Christmas yesterday with two of our boys' cousins, Drew and Ben. The four boys were close in age and have been good friends over the years. We have many fond memories of vacations, visits, and holidays spent together.

Watching the four of them grow up together was a gift. As little boys, they were just adorable. As they got older, they began to develop a witty banter that was so fun to observe. Of course, they were still adorable.

As we exchanged gifts, Bill asked everyone to pause and share a memory of Max when it was their turn. It felt like a good way to honor him in his absence.

It's almost impossible to believe we'll have to celebrate Christmas without him in all the years to come. We'll take vacations he won't be a part of. We'll visit each other, and he won't be with us.

We have a picture of the four of them taken about fifteen years ago. We were out to dinner, and they were sitting all together on a bench. They have their arms wrapped around each other and are making funny faces. Bill had them recreate this photo last Christmas. I am so thankful we have that photo as it's probably the last picture taken of the four of them together.

It's achingly painful to accept that life will go on without Max. His cousins will get married and have families of their own. There will be a new generation of cousins growing up together, taking vacations, celebrating holidays, and visiting each other. It makes me want to scream! I don't want other people's lives to stop because Max's life is over, but it is so unfair that he'll miss out on all of that.

"We'll take vacations he won't be a part of...visit each other, and he won't be with us."

Bill's closest friend is his brother, Tony. Drew and Ben are brothers and best friends. Sam lost his brother and best friend. When Sam gets married and has children, his kids won't have cousins to grow up with like Max and Sam did. I am heartbroken over all the lost opportunities.

I knew Christmas would be excruciating and opening gifts without him would be difficult, but what I didn't anticipate was the deep sorrow over what will never be.

Our world can be hard on those we view as "different".

One of my favorite Christmas memories of Max is from when he was about three years old. He had gotten "reindeer dust" from preschool that consisted of rolled oats mixed with glitter. His teachers told him to sprinkle it on our lawn so Santa could find our house.

He and I went out into the yard on that dark and cold Christmas Eve to throw it in the grass. I remember his sweet little face filled with wonder as he stared up into the sky looking for Santa's sleigh.

My sweet boy was full of wonder. He loved the fantastical and the magical. His favorite books were fantasy, and he read his first *Harry Potter* book between kindergarten and first grade.[12] We picked it up at a bookstore on a road trip, and he finished the entire novel within 24 hours. Another favorite was *The Inheritance Cycle* series about the dragon rider, Eragon.[13]

He was mesmerized by these magical worlds. I think he enjoyed reading about characters with special powers because he wished for special powers himself.

"We tout inclusion and diversity, but people are more comfortable when others are like them."

He was one of the most uniquely creative people I knew. He was a gifted writer himself and wrote stories, poetry, and songs. He wrote a short dystopian story just before his death, that he sent to his journalist cousin, Ryan, for feedback.

He wrote and recorded a rap song for his cousin, Mia, in recognition of her high school graduation in which he offered advice that he wished he had taken at her age. He also sketched and painted.

Max was one-of-a-kind. Yet, I think his talents and gifts made him feel a little outside the norm sometimes.

Our world can be hard on those we view as "different." As much as we tout inclusion and diversity, people are more comfortable when others are like them. When someone stands apart, I think too often we make them painfully aware of their differences because *we're* uncomfortable.

I am so grateful for all the ways in which Max stood apart. I'm glad he was such a uniquely gifted person. I am immensely proud to be his mom.

I think dealing with the death of a child qualifies as "walking through the valley of the shadow of death."

Psalm 23 is probably the most well-known psalm from the Bible. The line, "Even though I walk through the valley of the shadow of death, I will fear no evil..." (Psalm 23:4a NIV) is often quoted. I memorized this psalm several years ago. It's meant to bring comfort during a difficult time. It's meant to reassure us of God's presence when things seem chaotic. It's meant to remind us of God's goodness and love, despite our circumstances.

I am glad I know it, and I am glad I can recite it from memory, but it also makes me painfully aware of my own walk through the tragedy of losing Max. I think dealing with the death of a child qualifies as "walking through the valley of the shadow of death." It's good to remind myself that in this valley God is with me. It's good to remember God comforts me, and it's good to remember God is "preparing a table before me in the presence of my enemies." He's taking a really awful situation, which threatens to destroy me and He's sustaining me through it.

It is good to read those words and to recite them, even when they seem so difficult to grasp. My feelings are important, but they can be erratic and unpredictable. Even though I *feel* like God has abandoned me, this psalm reminds me that He hasn't. Even though I *feel* like this loss will overwhelm me, this psalm reminds me God will sustain me through it.

"He's taking a really awful situation...and He's sustaining me through it."

Max and I shared a love of books... a common passion.

Max loved books and read early. Even before he was reading, he was able to memorize his favorite books. In Preschool, he took one such book into school for Show and Tell. He regaled his teacher and classmates with his abilities to "read" this book from memory in front of his entire class. It was called *Cat Traps,* by Molly Coxe.[14] It was about a hungry cat looking for various types of snacks. The same line was repeated over and over throughout the book, "Cat wants a snack. Cat sets a trap. Cat gets a _______." Max truly loved this book. We read it over and over again, which is how he was able to memorize it.

He was always reading something, and as he got older it was difficult to find appropriate reading material to keep him entertained. Many times, I remember checking on him well after bedtime, only to find him still awake and reading. He was so inquisitive.

For Christmas last year, he got all of us books. As usual, he was thoughtful in his selections. He bought me a classic book I had talked about reading for years, as well as a debut novel by a new author. In past years he had given me cookbooks and gardening books as he knew how much I loved to do both.

During college, he majored in English and Philosophy, mostly because of his love of books. Although we had interests in different genres, Max and I shared a love of books. I am thankful for that common passion.

Christmas...not just a day to get through but an entire season.

It's Christmas morning, and I miss Max so much, it's hard to breathe. This Christmas has been so difficult. It's not just a day to get through but an entire season. Over the last few weeks, the thought that's been replaying in my head like a ticker tape is, "I'm desperately unhappy, desperately unhappy, desperately unhappy."

Everywhere I turn there are reminders of Max, such as Christmas ornaments he made and Christmas books we read together when he was little. In preschool, he made a craft with Christmas trees by using his sweet little handprints. I couldn't bear to hang our Christmas stockings this year. Ours hanging there without his, or worse, hanging his and it remaining empty, would have been too painful.

His birthday back in September and Thanksgiving Day were both tough to handle, but they were each just one day. I was able to prepare myself and create a plan to get through the day. Christmas has been a completely different experience. Over and over again are situations in which his absence is profoundly felt, and we have more Christmas gatherings to attend.

"Over and over again are situations in which his absence is profoundly felt, and we still have more Christmas gatherings to attend."

I wish he had known how desperately we would miss him this Christmas. I wish he had known how much I would miss his thoughtful gifts and sitting with him Christmas morning and talking. I wish he had known how much I would miss his sense of humor and unique perspective on the world and how much I miss hugging and kissing him. "I miss my sweet boy, I miss my sweet boy, I miss my sweet boy." Another ticker tape running through my head.

I know how fleeting those seasons can be...I am going to try to savor those precious moments of calm.

I came across a Christmas photo from 2005. The four of us and Cookie, our darling little Cairn Terrier, are standing in front of a Christmas tree at my parent's house. Cookie is six months old and was the second most stubborn one in the family. Sam had the distinction of winning that title. Bill coined the term "stu-nnoying" (stubborn + annoying) for him because he had perfected the art of annoying his older brother. Max was playing pee-wee football in what would prove for him an uncharacteristic, organized sports phase. My handsome hubby had hair. I was in the midst of a decade where I look surprised and shocked in all photos. My parents were healthy and literally the best grandparents on the planet.

It was a season of peace and happiness. Did I appreciate it? And if I did, did I also assume things would always stay this way? Probably. Of course, now I know how fleeting those seasons can be, and I am going to try to savor those precious moments of calm.

"It was a season of peace and happiness. Did I appreciate it?"

According to one study, a link was found between higher IQ and mood disorders.

"Some of dis kinda" (some of this kind)

"I don't ike" (I do not like)

"Panpake" (pancake)

"Go, kids! Go, go, go, kids!"

"Don't know. Don't care."

These are just a few Maxisms, phrases he said as a child, that Bill and I continue to use to this day. Because he began talking so early, he said some pretty hilarious things. I loved when we were able to have real conversations because I so appreciated this glimpse into his young mind.

continued on next page

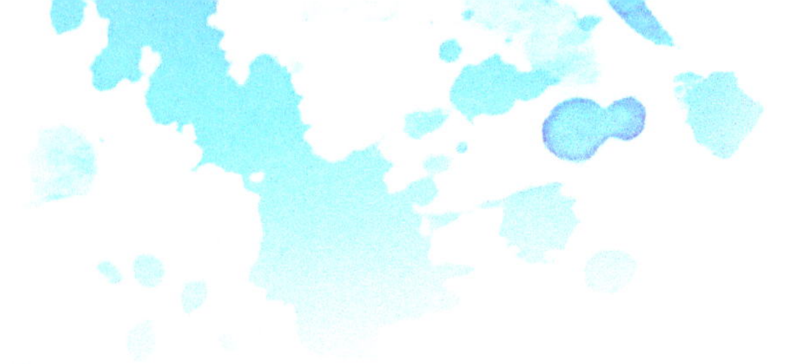

They say early talking is NOT a sign of intelligence. People use Albert Einstein as an example to support this theory. Apparently, Einstein didn't speak until he was about four years old. I, for one, don't buy it. My Max was wickedly smart, and I believe his early speech was a sign of this intelligence.

Perhaps if he had been less intelligent, he would not have been so troubled. I don't know. Is there a correlation between intelligence and mental illness? According to one study, a link was found between higher IQ and mood disorders. In the general population, 10 percent suffer from mood disorders and 10 percent from anxiety disorders. In those with higher IQs, the percentages jump to 27 and 20, respectively. Sobering statistics.[15] However, I guess if Max had been less intelligent, he would not have been himself.

I am so sorry his brilliant mind was most likely a source of pain for him, but I loved it, nonetheless.

"I am so sorry his brilliant mind was most likely a source of pain for him, but I loved it, nonetheless."

We cherish the painting... it truly captures his unique essence.

My sister and brother-in-law gave us a painting of Max for Christmas. They have an artist friend who combined two drastically different pictures of Max into one painting. The first picture is just a headshot of Max smiling into the camera. The second is a picture of him from the Pittsburgh protest dressed all in black.

My brother-in-law told us that he loved the dichotomy of those two pictures. In the first, Max looks like a clean-cut, buttoned-up, conventional guy. In the second, he looks like a bad-ass activist. Both are accurate portrayals of him.

Max had many different looks over the years. He had long hair, short hair, and buzz cuts. He tried to dye his dark hair blonde a few years ago, but the finished product was more orange than blonde. He got many tattoos over the years. He loved traditional menswear but also baggy t-shirts and sweats. His signature look was his pair of raw denim jeans with a black, hooded sweatshirt. He wore these jeans so frequently that they had the outline of his wallet in the back pocket and his phone in the front pocket. We've kept those jeans, and I don't believe I will ever part with them.

He also had an orange camouflage winter coat he wore frequently. I thought it was rather hideous, but Max loved it. Once he got into a verbal spat with a guy on the street who threatened to "Beat yo' ass and steal yo' coat!"

Max had a unique taste in clothing from a young age. When he was two, he wore his snow boots for an entire summer. That was the same summer he had a hard time transitioning from sweatpants and jeans to shorts. We finally convinced him to wear shorts with his snow boots. We had to pick our battles. We cherish the painting of Max given to us by Kelly and Rocco because it truly captures his unique essence.

...we all felt compelled to make a change...celebrating the traditional way would've been too painful.

Every year we celebrate Christmas with dear family friends. Typically, everyone gathers at our house for a meal, games, and a gift exchange. It was a day we all looked forward to, and nobody more than Max.

This year we all felt compelled to make a change, as celebrating the traditional way would have been too painful without Max.

We decided to go bowling instead, and we had a blast! Bowling with little kids is equal parts hilarious and frustrating. As usual, we laughed a lot with this beautiful family.

When we exchanged gifts, they gave us the most thoughtful gifts imaginable.

They had blankets made for each of us, printed with a picture of our beloved Max. My blanket is a sweet picture of Max, Sam, and me taken at the beach. Bill's blanket is a picture of Max and him taken in Italy. Sam's blanket is a beautiful picture of Max and him hugging.

Many people have made beautiful gestures like this since Max passed. I don't know how we would have survived these last months without the care, support, and love of our friends and family. We are truly blessed by them.

"Many people have made beautiful gestures like this since Max passed.

I don't know how we would have survived these last months without the care, support, and love of our friends and family.

We are truly blessed by them."

A Celebration of Life in Photos

November & December

re-creation of funny faces (Max, Sam, and Cousins)

winnie the pooh: Max's favorite

Max's Christmas angel, 2000

Pop-Pop Ed's Xmas Card

Family Christmas Pic, 2005

Erin + Max, Thanksgiving, 2017

Max with "genius babies"

Max at protest, 2020

Painting from Sister & Hubby

bumblebee sketch for Sam

Comedy Clubs where Max Performed

new year
new reality

JANUARY THROUGH MARCH

We have all heard love is an action and not just a feeling, and perhaps hope is the same.

I am so glad to say goodbye to 2020. It has been a brutal year. As I reflect upon the loss of our sweet Max, I'm struck by the hopelessness I've felt since he passed. My prayers for healing went unanswered. My dreams for him will never come true. My desire to see him thrive will not become a reality.

Hope is a funny thing. Bill has a book titled, *Hope is Not a Strategy: The 6 Keys to Winning the Complex Sale,* by Rick Page.[16] The premise is that in sales you need to have a plan of action, that action is more important than words, and careful planning is more valuable than ideas. I've always loved that title because it highlights how most of us view hope as just a feeling or a way of wishful thinking. Shouldn't those of us who call ourselves Christians, view hope differently? Shouldn't our hope be more focused on trust and confidence in God?

Yes, I've *felt* hopeless since Max passed. Yes, I pray I will once again *feel* hopeful. I'm beginning to realize though that hope is much more than a feeling, it's an action too. Perhaps when I'm feeling hopeless, I can turn to Jesus and proclaim that He CAN and WILL change my feelings. I don't need to assume I will always feel this way. Instead, I can say, "This isn't the way things should be." I can say, "Jesus YOU can turn this around," and then I can wait expectantly for Him to do it and know that my feelings will change. We have all heard love is an action and not just a feeling, and perhaps hope is the same. Here's to "hoping" 2021 is better than 2020.

...the dormant plants, shrubs, and trees seem to mirror my own dormant heart.

One of the things that gets me out of bed is walking dates with friends, and I have one scheduled on most days. Walking in nature while talking with a friend is good for my mind, body, and soul. I have one friend so willing to walk with me that I think she would say yes even if I called her at midnight. Walking is meditative. Friends are restorative. I cannot imagine getting through the last few months without either one.

The exercise helps me breathe when I feel like I am suffocating. The beauty of nature inspires me. Now it's winter and my walks are not quite as enjoyable. While the winter landscape is still beautiful, the dormant plants, shrubs, and trees seem to mirror my own dormant heart.

That is part of the reason I am already looking forward to returning to Florida. The sunshine and color are a welcome change from the cold and gray landscape of Pittsburgh in the winter.

"I've felt hopeless since he passed. I pray I will once again feel hopeful."

"Consider it pure joy, my brothers, when you face trials of many kinds..."

(JAMES 1:2A NIV)

I listened to a podcast yesterday about finding joy in the midst of pain. On the surface, this sounds impossible. When we're in deep pain, joy seems like the least likely emotion. There's a verse in the book of James I have always found deeply challenging. "Consider it pure joy, my brothers, when you face trials of many kinds..." (James 1:2a NIV)

I remember the first time I read those words, I thought, "That's the dumbest thing I have ever heard!" Why on earth would I consider a trial "pure joy?" It doesn't make sense: it's not natural.

While Max was struggling, I began to have a little appreciation for this truth. Despite his and our suffering, I was able to see some glimmer of growth and maturity in my life. I felt close to God through prayer and Bible study and my faith remained strong and steadfast.

In the days following his death, we were surrounded by dear friends and family. As we wept and cried out about the unfairness of his untimely death, we also shared memories and stories that made us laugh aloud. I was able to see joy in the midst of pain.

I don't understand how joy and pain can exist simultaneously, but I'm thankful that they can. I believe it's another example of God's grace. He knows how hard and beautiful life can be, and that we will experience both joy and pain. He gives us mercies each and every day to handle what comes across our path. I am thankful for His presence, His providence, and His provision.

...when we're in a season of grief and healing, we have permission to prioritize our healing.

2020 was brutal. Not only did we lose Max, but the world also seemed to fall apart. There was a global pandemic, racial and social unrest, one of the ugliest presidential election campaigns in recent history, and much more.

It would be impossible to prevent all those issues from impacting my grief. Rather, they have served to shorten my fuse considerably and made me less able to remain engaged in some relationships. I'm learning that I can't fully trust some people with my grief. Not everyone in my circle is safe for me right now. And for my own survival, I'm realizing that I need to guard my heart and prioritize my healing.

We all have people in our lives who require more grace than others. It's just the way it is, and that's okay. But I'm not the same person now and I simply cannot engage in the same way that I was able to in the past.

I guess what I'm getting at is that when we're in a season of grief and healing, we have permission to prioritize our healing. For other codependents out there, our needs are important too, and self-care is not selfish.

After we lost Max, a friend told us, "You get a free pass for a year. You can do anything you want." I'm taking that advice to heart, but it's hard sometimes. As moms, we're accustomed to putting the needs of others ahead of our own, sometimes to our detriment. It is a challenging lesson to learn, that my needs matter too.

Those early years set the stage for the way Sam responded when Max got sick.

I am beginning to realize what a special relationship Max and Sam shared. They certainly had their share of disagreements and annoyances, but ultimately they were great friends.

It started when I was pregnant with Sam. Max was fascinated by the idea of a baby growing in my "belly." One evening while I was making dinner, he asked, "Mommy, how did the baby get in your belly?" I said, "Well, Mommies have eggs and Daddies have seeds. When the egg and seed get together, they make a baby." Max thought for a moment and responded, "How about when my dad gets home, you show me how?" I have told that sweet story more times than I can count. Even at almost three years of age, he was a curious and deep thinker.

During my pregnancy, we read a special book over and over about becoming a big brother in an effort to help prepare Max for his new role. In the book, the big brother welcomed a baby sister into their family and took seriously his responsibility to look out for her. Max took the lessons in this book to heart.

When we brought Sam home from the hospital, the only negative thing Max said was, "But I wanted a girl baby." Despite this, Max quickly adjusted to having a little brother. Sam loved his big brother. Whenever Max was around, Sam would watch him with laser focus and laugh at everything Max did. As they got older, Max took on his role as Sam's protector. He intervened when he felt Sam was treated unfairly and stood up for him when necessary.

I guess those early years set the stage for the way Sam responded when Max got sick. In a sense, Max's health issues took over our family. He struggled for so many years, and he was never far from my thoughts. I was preoccupied with his suffering.

"He struggled for so many years, and he was never far from my thoughts."

Sam could have been resentful and angry. He could have felt ignored or marginalized, but he didn't. I remember giving him an article about how to deal with a family member who lived with mental illness. This article detailed the challenges to the other family members and compared our experience to a roller coaster ride: constant ups and downs. I could certainly relate.

Sam told me after reading the article, "This isn't about me, Mom. It's about Max, and how we can support him." What a thoughtful and compassionate response! I am so thankful for their close relationship. I know Sam misses Max, but I am forever grateful for the bond they shared in this life.

How fortunate we were to witness such a beautiful relationship between brothers.

As I continue to contemplate the relationship Max and Sam shared, I am reminded of a situation that further reinforces Max's concern and protectiveness towards his little brother.

When Sam was about two, we transitioned him from a crib to a "big boy bed." He was a very active toddler, so I looked forward to putting him down for the night, particularly when Bill was traveling for work. Unfortunately, Sam took advantage of no longer being behind bars and would get out of bed. Every. Single. Night.

continued on next page

One night at my wit's end, I said to Sam, "If you get out of bed again, I will reverse the knob on your door and lock you in your room." He obviously didn't think I would follow through, so of course, he got out of bed. Again.

I calmly got a screwdriver from the toolbox and began to remove his doorknob. During this episode, Max was crying from his own room, "Mom, please don't lock him in. What if there's a fire?" I was not deterred and continued my efforts as Sam cried, "She's doing it, Max. She's really doing it!"

I know, not my finest parenting moment. I never had to actually reverse the knob and lock Sam in. I think the trauma of the experience was enough for both of them.

The point is that Max took his role as big brother and protector quite seriously. I think many brothers would have been gleeful about their little brother "getting it" or at the very least unconcerned about a punishment that did not include them. Not Max. He was a sensitive and loving brother from beginning to end. How fortunate Sam was to have such a caring big brother even if it was for only a short time. How fortunate we were to witness such a beautiful relationship between brothers.

"I know now that my effort didn't address the real causes for his own struggles, and they were just temporary solutions."

...the opposite of depression is NOT happiness, it's motivation.

It is another cold, gray, gloomy day in Pittsburgh. Although I love this city, the weather here, during the winter, is truly awful. The summers and autumns are lovely, but right around Thanksgiving the clouds roll in and stay until Easter. It's amazing how the lack of sun can affect my mood. These gray days mirror my feelings. Seasonal Affective Disorder is real.

The weather affected Max too. He really struggled during the winter months in Pittsburgh. I did all I could to help him. I gave him a therapy lamp that mimics sunlight. I bought him Vitamin D to take during the winter. In the unlikely event we had a sunny winter day, I would call him and say, "Go outside and soak up the sun."

I know now that my efforts didn't address the real causes for his own struggles, and they were just temporary solutions.

One of his therapists told us that the opposite of depression is NOT happiness, it's motivation. When someone is in a depressive state, they lack the motivation to do even the most basic things. I understand that lack of motivation now in a way I never did before.

But I will sit under my therapy lamp and continue to take my vitamin D because I know I should. Sometimes a "should" gets me through the day.

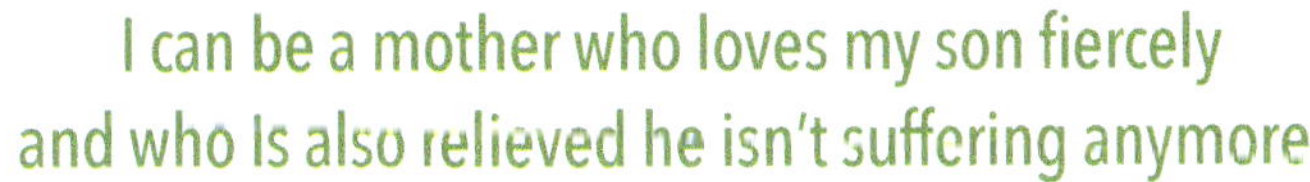

I can be a mother who loves my son fiercely and who is also relieved he isn't suffering anymore.

I had a conversation yesterday, with a friend who is suffering from depression. I don't know if the cause is circumstantial, weather-related, or chemical in nature. What I do know is that talking to her was reminiscent of talking to Max: the same flat affect, the same monotone voice, the same lack of interest or excitement in anything. Trying to get her to engage was like pulling teeth.

I have noticed that when I'm around someone who is guarded or reserved for whatever reason, I feel like I need to be animated and enthusiastic for both of us. It's exhausting for me and probably highly annoying to them.

My conversation yesterday brought back all the conversations I had with Max when he was struggling, and God forgive me, it gave me a sense of relief that I won't have those conversations with him ever again. The relief I've felt since his death is a source of guilt. Isn't it wrong to feel relief, and shouldn't I only feel sadness and loss? Again and again, I feel like a terrible mother.

I guess I am starting to understand that relief and sadness can coexist. I don't have to feel just one or the other, I can actually feel both. That's a comforting thought. It goes against my "black and white," "good or bad" binary thinking.

"I can miss him so much it hurts, and still love the people in my life passionately."

Life is hard, but it's also wonderful. Living in the tension of this reality is tough and, in a way, counterintuitive. I think it boils down to self-compassion. I can be a mother who loves my son fiercely and who is also relieved he isn't suffering anymore. And relieved that I don't have to suffer along with him any longer. I can be a person deeply grieving the loss of my beautiful boy and also enjoying the beauty of the life I still have. I can miss Max so much it hurts, and still love the people in my life passionately.

I'm learning that these seemingly polar opposites can be true at the same time, and I am thankful for this lesson.

He understood things and felt things more deeply than anyone else I know. I imagine the world is a very difficult place for people like him.

In the last week, I've heard of two suicides: one was a twenty-five-year-old man and the other, God help us, a seventh-grade girl. I can't help but think we are living through an epidemic of suicide.

I don't know about the twenty-five-year-old man, but I know the seventh-grade girl was highly intelligent and a gifted student at her school. Max was also gifted. The teacher who told me about this young girl also told me about the differences she has observed in gifted students, throughout her years of teaching. She claims that truly gifted kids with an exceptionally high IQ really see the world differently. They have an ability to grasp events and situations at a deeper level and a younger age than others. What a burden this must be!

continued on next page

I know this was the case for Max. He understood things and felt things more deeply than anyone else I know. I imagine the world is a very difficult place for people like him.

As much as I hate to admit it, I'm so thankful he doesn't have to experience this broken world anymore. Things in our country and world were bad when he passed, but they are even worse now. Max would be in a desperate state if he were still here. This may sound callous and unfathomable for a mother to say, but I know his passing has spared my sweet boy additional pain. I'm incredibly thankful he is indeed spared.

Rather than saying someone "committed" suicide, we should say they "died by suicide."

I've learned so much since our sweet Max passed. One of the most important things I've learned is about the terminology we use when talking about suicide. Rather than saying someone "committed" suicide, we should say they "died by suicide."

The word "committed" has very different connotations. It implies the carrying out of or perpetrating a mistake, a crime, or an immoral act. While suicide is terrible, it shouldn't be in the same category as criminal or immoral actions.

"While suicide is terrible, it shouldn't be in the same category as criminal or immoral actions."

I've started to change my language and say that Max "died by suicide." I was talking to someone yesterday who lost a loved one to suicide and, several times during our conversation, she stated her family member, "committed suicide." That language was jarring and disturbing to hear.

I owe this realization to speaker and author, Kayla Stoecklein, who lost her husband to suicide. She says when someone dies of a heart attack we don't say he/she, "committed a heart attack." The same should be true of death by suicide.

"Like so many other things related to mental illness, we need to change the way we view and talk about suicide."

Like so many other things related to mental illness, we need to change the way we view and talk about suicide. I know Max wasn't himself on the night he ended his life. I know he was in such severe pain, he just needed it to stop. Of course, I'm devastated by his choice, and I'm so very grateful he is no longer suffering. I'm learning I can be both devastated and grateful, sad and relieved, hopeless and yet hopeful.

My therapist has encouraged me to eliminate the word "but" from my vocabulary; to replace any "but" with an "and." It's tough to do AND I'm trying.

It's comforting for me to know I may be helping others through their own valley of darkness.

Facebook has become my support group. I know that sounds strange since the platform is full of venomous political and social rants, multi-level marketing business opportunities, and product advertisements directly targeted at me. Despite all these things, it has become a source of support, encouragement, and healing for me.

When Max died, my therapist encouraged me to journal in order to get my thoughts and feelings out. Over the months, I have written reflections of things I've discovered and learned as well as many memories of my sweet boy. Some of these reflections and memories I've also posted on Facebook.

The response has been overwhelming. I often receive such positive feedback from people some of whom I haven't seen in 20 years or more. Their kind words and support help me to feel seen and heard.

Several people have told me they've forwarded my posts to friends or family members who are also dealing with loss and grief. Although these people may not be in the same situation as I am, loss is universal. At some point in life, we will all have to deal with loss, whether it's loss of a loved one, a relationship, a job, etc. It's comforting for me to know I may be helping others through their own valley of darkness.

I'm thankful for an outlet like Facebook which allows me to share my insights, reflections, pain, and joys. I'm even more thankful for all the people who continue to offer me support, encouragement, validation, and love via this platform.

I pray I can continue to practice self-compassion when these negative thoughts enter my mind.

I met with an acquaintance yesterday who reached out to me after Max passed. She told me she understood a little of what we were dealing with through personal experience. She offered to get together and talk if ever I wanted.

During our time together she shared that she has a son who also lives with significant mental illness. Her son is in his early forties. He is able to live on his own but doesn't work. He receives disability and financial support from his parents. She said he doesn't have a social life because he doesn't have much in common with other people his age. She and her husband are his only support system.

She explained that she lives with fear and worry every day. She's afraid he will end his life, she's worried about his future, and she's deeply concerned about what will happen to him when she's gone.

After I left her, I felt a tremendous sense of relief that our day-to-day worry about Max is gone. I'm relieved we aren't consumed with fear about Max's future. I'm relieved he won't be suffering into middle age the way this woman's son is suffering.

continued on next page

I thought dealing with Max's issues for more than eight years was tough. This poor woman has been dealing with her son's struggles for more than twenty years. The sense of relief I felt upon hearing her story was of course followed by feelings of guilt and shame. What a terrible person I must be for feeling grateful that I'm not in her shoes anymore. What a terrible mother for being relieved my son is gone. I know these feelings are probably completely normal and natural given what we've been through. My closest friends have told me so. I pray I can continue to practice self-compassion when these negative thoughts enter my mind.

He does indeed see me, understands the magnitude of my pain and sadness, and is with me through it all.

A friend sent me a gospel song this morning. It's titled, "I Understand," by Smokie Norful.[17] It's about the assurance that God is with us while we walk through our valleys, that He sees us and understands what we're going through. What a beautiful and comforting reminder.

It's a reminder I need as I navigate the darkest valley of my life. I've felt abandoned by God and distant from Him. I've felt angry at Him. This song helps me remember that He does indeed see me, understands the magnitude of my pain and sadness, and is with me through it all. I needed this reminder today.

When our children are little, we tell them what to think. We fool ourselves into thinking we can control their opinions, beliefs, and values.

We're all probably familiar with the phrase, "Let there be peace on earth and let it begin with me" which is the first line in a song written by Jill Jackson-Miller and Sy Miller in 1955. I heard an interesting twist on this phrase the other day that seems to reflect the attitude of many people, "Let there be peace on earth and let it begin with y'all." I laughed when I heard it because it sounds so ridiculous. Unfortunately, there is much truth behind it.

Most of us want things to change in our world, but we don't want to be the ones to make a change. I think we really want other people to change to be more like us and think more like we do. Then once we all think alike and agree, there can be peace, right? Good luck with that!

I remember many conversations with Max where we fundamentally disagreed on a topic. Usually, it was a topic we both felt very strongly about, and neither of us was willing to budge. I remember telling a friend that every time he and I were together he said something that offended one of my deeply held beliefs.

"Max opened my eyes to things I didn't know…he helped me realize the change I wanted to see needed to begin with me."

When our children are little, we tell them what to think. We fool ourselves into thinking we can control their opinions, beliefs, and values. At some point, we learn this is not true. They are individuals with their own minds, their own wills, and their own passions. Max taught us this at an earlier age than most.

I remember him arguing his point with teachers, family members, and even strangers while he was still in elementary school. The mother of one of his fourth-grade friends once told me, "He knows a little bit about everything." How right she was.

Over time, I learned to listen to him more when we saw things differently. He opened my eyes to things I didn't know. Often, he helped me realize the change I wanted to see needed to begin with me. He helped me understand I didn't have all the answers just because I was the mother. Max taught me a lot in life, and he continues to teach me things in death. I'm thankful for his influence.

At a young age, he saw most things the way they were.

When Max was little, he had a best friend, named Joey. Joey lived next door and he was three months younger than Max. They were beautiful little boys. Max had olive skin and big dark eyes, and Joey was fair with blond hair and blue eyes. Those two were inseparable! They played together almost every day, and one day, they were out on our new rope hammock. We had it hanging on trees between our two yards, and they were climbing on it and swinging it wildly.

I went outside to tell them to be careful. I told them, "You two are going to put a hole in that thing!" Max looked at me, looked back at the hammock, and replied, "Mom, it's full of holes!" Even at a young age, he saw most things the way they were. We used to claim he was an old soul. My mom used to joke, "He's been here before." He was just a special little guy who grew into a special young man.

We've been told that God especially entrusted him to us. This sentiment is equal parts comforting and disheartening.

Today is eight months since we lost Max. In some ways, it seems like just yesterday, and in other ways, it seems like a lifetime ago. Regardless, this day is hitting me harder than the previous months. Maybe it's because the disbelief and numbness have worn off. Maybe reality is finally setting in that our loss is permanent.

The baby boy of friends was born on the day we lost Max. Every month they post pictures of him as he grows. He's a beautiful, fat baby just like Max was. He has huge eyes and a big, round, bald head like Max had. Seeing photos of this precious baby is bittersweet. Naturally, we're thrilled for these friends because we know the joy a baby brings to a family. We're also sad because every month it's a reminder of what we've lost.

I've been looking through pictures of young Max. He was truly beautiful! Looking at his sweet face and knowing all the struggles he would face as he grew up, fills me with sorrow.

People have told us both before and after he died, that we were exactly the parents Max needed. We've been told that God especially entrusted him to us. This sentiment is equal parts comforting and disheartening. I think about all the ways we failed him over the years and try to balance it with all the ways we loved and fought for him. In some ways, I'm relieved the fight is over, and in other ways, I wish like hell I could fight for him one more time!

The past eight months have been the most difficult of my life. I've been living in my darkest valley. I've experienced regret, despair, sadness, hopelessness, and yes, also glimmers of joy. I believe, as time goes on, I will have more glimmers of joy, but for today, I miss my Max more than I can ever express.

I think that's the hardest lesson to learn as a parent, that we can't fix all things for our children.

Words are so inadequate. Many people have expressed this to us since we lost Max. I've heard numerous times, "There are no words!" and I agree.

I've been writing since we lost him to try and make sense of my swirling thoughts and emotions. I've been trying to articulate my feelings, and it's just so difficult. I find myself searching for the right adjectives to fully capture and describe how I'm feeling, but there just aren't words to describe the depths of my pain and sorrow.

How can I put into words the loss of something so precious and beloved? How can I, as a mother, express my deep heartache at losing my son? How can I look at pictures of his beautiful face and accept that I will not hug or kiss him again in this life? How can I reconcile his pain and struggles with the presence of deep love in his life, in our family?

There were so many times I felt helpless while he was alive; helpless that I couldn't take away his pain, couldn't make him better, and couldn't fix things for him. I think that's the hardest lesson to learn as a parent, that we can't fix all things for our children. When they're little, we fool ourselves into thinking we have far more control than we actually do. As they grow, we realize that's just an illusion.

I find myself wanting to warn young moms, to grab them, shake them, and scream, "Don't fool yourself!" I want them to realize their child is a gift. I want them to realize they cannot protect their child from most things in life. I want them to know that every messy moment spent with their child is precious.

A few years ago, I was introduced to two young moms. The first was the "I have it all together" mom. She talked about the strict schedule she kept with her kids for naps, bedtime, meals, snacks, and play. She was quietly smug and confident in her role as a mom. The second mom was distraught because her young son wasn't eating properly. She was struggling because she felt like she was failing at something so basic and simple.

I remember writing the struggling mom a note to encourage her. I remember saying that she was learning an important and valuable lesson early in the lives of her children, that she wasn't actually in control. I told her that as her children grew, there would be many things outside of her control and the best thing she could do was to love them and care for them, but ultimately to surrender them to the Lord.

"...love them and care for them, but ultimately surrender them to the Lord."

I don't recall if I ever talked to her or heard from her after writing this note. She probably threw it in the trash thinking it was hogwash. I know I probably would have done so in her shoes. It took LOTS of heartache for me to learn I wasn't in control of my sweet Max. I wish I had been less stubborn and prideful.

You WILL have trouble.

We met a couple recently who have experienced so much suffering and tragedy in the past several years. Both the woman's parents died from cancer within just a few months of each other. The man's mother developed Alzheimer's, and they cared for her around the clock for more than five years. After all this, the woman herself was diagnosed with a rare and very painful form of cancer. She's had radiation, chemotherapy, and surgery and has undergone painful examinations and treatments, all in an effort to eradicate the disease. They live with the constant fear her cancer will return.

It's tempting, when meeting people like this, to compare suffering. I heard someone call it the Olympics of Suffering, the competition to determine who receives the gold medal in suffering. It's natural to say, "Our situation is bad, but their situation is worse." Or, to say, "Although it's hard to lose a parent, it doesn't even compare to losing a child."

Why do we play the comparison game? Perhaps it's a way to make ourselves feel better, or perhaps it's a way to justify our feelings of unfairness and self-pity. I'm beginning to realize everyone has hardship. It reminds me of the Bible verse, John 16:33b, "Here on earth you *will* have many trials and sorrows. But take heart, because I have overcome the world." (John 16:33b NIV)

This verse doesn't say, "you may have" trouble but "you WILL have" trouble. Nobody gets through this life unscathed. It's easy to look at the carefully cultivated image others project and think they have it easy, but it's simply not true. EVERYBODY has difficulties in this life, it's just a question of when they will occur.

Hopefully, our trials and sorrows serve to make us more compassionate, more authentic, and more human. I think these are the qualities God would want us to demonstrate in our pain.

Depression is a disease like diabetes or heart disease.

Family was very important to Max. As he got older, he realized just how unique our family was. Bill and I have a strong marriage. Max and Sam grew up with grandparents, aunts and uncles, and cousins as a big part of their lives. Max met many friends over the years whose parents were divorced and many who didn't have any extended family they saw regularly. He was grateful for our large, close family.

We took annual family beach vacations over the years. I'm so grateful for the cherished memories of these happy times. Max loved his cousins deeply, and, as the oldest grandchild on my side of the family, he felt protective of them. One of his very best friends throughout his life was his cousin, Michael. They were born just a few months apart, and they shared a close and special relationship.

Because of his own struggles, Max often attracted those who were struggling themselves. I used to say he was a wounded bird who attracted other wounded birds. As he matured, I believe he realized his struggles could have been more difficult if, like many of his friends, his formative years had been more tumultuous due to difficult family dynamics.

continued on next page

I believe he viewed our family as a source of comfort and safety, which was why he was able to return home to rest and regroup when he needed to. Although these instances were worrisome and uncomfortable knowing he was in the midst of great suffering, I'm incredibly thankful he mostly viewed our home and family as a respite.

I know that his depression wasn't circumstantial. I know depression is a disease like diabetes or heart disease. But, just like those illnesses, depression can be exacerbated by lifestyle factors. As much as we all wanted a miraculous cure, it didn't happen. However, we did feel he was on an upward trajectory of self-care when COVID hit.

I don't know if things would have ended differently if the pandemic and resulting isolation had not occurred. Perhaps it would have simply postponed the inevitable. I do know that none of us could have predicted the devastation and heartache of this past year for so many, including our own profound devastation. We miss our sweet Max and desperately wish things had turned out differently.

Living with mental illness is to live with constant background noise.

We got our first family dog, Cookie, in August 2005. She was an adorable, little Cairn Terrier we had shipped from Nebraska. We picked her out from a breeder on the Internet. We didn't know anything about the breeder, the conditions at the facility, or anything about the temperament of her mother or father. All we knew was that she was a darling, little puppy. We broke every rule in the dog adoption book.

Cookie arrived by plane on a hot August afternoon. We had to go to the airport to pick her up. A friend of Max's commented

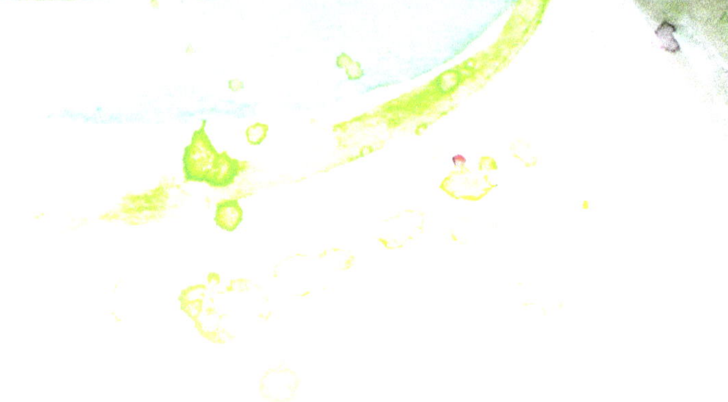

at the time, "Do you mean to tell me you couldn't find a single dog in the whole state of Pennsylvania?"

She was a four-and-a-half-pound ball of fur, and we all fell instantly in love. We decided to name her Cookie Evelyn Blechman. Her middle name, Evelyn, was Max's idea. He thought since he and Sam had important-sounding middle names, she should too.

Cookie quickly grew into a feisty, stubborn puppy. She attacked all the boy's stuffed animals and gouged out their eyes. We installed an invisible dog fence on our property from which she regularly escaped. More times than I can recount, Max, Sam, and I would go searching for her through the woods, calling, "Cook, Cook, Cook!"

Looking back on those episodes, I can see the early manifestation of Max's mental health issues. While Sam and I would be anxious to find her, Max's anxiety was at a different level altogether. As we combed the woods for signs of her, Max would cry inconsolably. He would lament, "What if we can't find her? What if she gets hit by a car? What if another animal attacks her?" I would say, "Honey, let's just find her. Everything will be okay."

Max experienced things differently. That's part of what made him compassionate and caring, but it was also a source of pain for him. His mind seemed to be consumed by anxiety and fear.

I recently heard that living with mental illness is to live with constant background noise. It's like trying to go through normal, daily activities with a noise you can't tune out. This must be exhausting. I remember often thinking that Max was lost in his own head, and I guess he really was. I compared him to the quintessential absent-minded professor, but perhaps he was just distracted by a persistent noise in his head.

I'm certain that noise has ceased now that he's gone. I'm thankful he doesn't have to deal with the continuous darkness, anxiety, and fear he lived with in this life. I'm so sorry he's gone AND so thankful he isn't suffering anymore.

His many advantages in life couldn't protect him from the ravages of mental illness.

Last night Bill and I watched a TV show that depicted the devastation of death and the unparalleled joys of birth. It was a vivid reminder for us of both of those events in Max's life.

I remember the overwhelming joy of his birth. We fell in love with him the moment we held him in our arms. He was a beautiful baby, and we were filled with hopes and dreams for his future. As he got a bit older and his intelligence began to reveal itself, we grew even more confident in the promise of his future. He was a beautiful and compassionate boy growing up in an upper-middle-class, traditional family. He attended excellent schools, was active in our church, participated in various activities, and was surrounded by a loving and supportive family. In other words, he had the textbook "perfect" upbringing.

The fact that his many advantages in life couldn't protect him from the ravages of mental illness, speak to the insidious nature of this disease. It also helps to explain why we and others had a hard time accepting his struggles. After all, he seemed to enjoy every advantage a child could have.

As he got older and sicker, I had to grieve the loss of my hopes and dreams for him. I was disappointed when he dropped out

"As he got older and sicker, I had to grieve the loss of my hopes and dreams for him."

of college. I was stricken when he lost job after job due to his depression and epilepsy. I was devastated when he lost his faith. I was consumed with fear over his future.

All of that pales in comparison to the grief I've felt since he passed. While he was still alive, I was able to maintain a semblance of hope. Now that hope is gone; he's gone and it's final.

In the TV show we were watching, a couple of the characters swam out into the middle of a lake and screamed. It was a way to let out their grief, guilt, and other emotions. They were carrying around these overwhelming feelings which were eating them alive. After screaming in the lake, they felt lighter, maybe a bit freer from the weight of their grief. Maybe I'll give it a try.

...all shock and denial have worn off.

After Max passed, several people gave us wind chimes in memory of him. I'm sitting here listening to one of the wind chimes right now. It is a soothing sound, and it reminds me of my special boy. I'd much prefer the sound of his voice though. I'd rather talk to him than simply remember him.

As the nine-month anniversary of his passing approaches, I'm struck by the finality of his death. I guess all shock and denial have worn off, and all I'm left with is the devastating loss. Over these last nine months, I've learned many customs of death that I didn't know before. I guess up until now I've been fortunate

continued on next page

when it comes to death. I've lost grandparents and a few other loved ones, but nothing compares to the pain of losing Max.

When an older person passes, it's hard but not completely unexpected. We're often able to celebrate a long life well-lived. We didn't have that chance with Max. When I think about his death, all I can see is promise and potential snuffed out. I see a life cut too short. I see a sensitive, intelligent, handsome, and loving young man, gone forever. No soothing sound can take away the pain and reality of this loss.

It feels almost disrespectful to keep on living.

I'm reading Michelle Obama's book, *Becoming.*[18] She describes losing her father after years of him battling Multiple Sclerosis. She talks about how much it hurts to live after someone has died. She rightfully points out that everything feels frivolous and inappropriate.

I couldn't agree more. So many things have felt trivial and unimportant since Max passed. For example, arguments and disagreements between people grate on my nerves, as they seem so petty in light of what we've been through.

Another thing I'm struggling with is that it feels almost disrespectful to keep on living, have fun, and enjoy life. There's a part of me that died the day he did, and it sits in judgment when the other part of me seems to be getting on with life. I know this is wrong. I know Max wouldn't want me to feel this way, but as usual, there's a disconnect between my head and my heart.

I had a conversation recently, where someone pointed out how nice it is that Max is still teaching and growing me since his death. I hope I can learn what I need to learn and grow in the ways necessary, but honestly, I'd just rather have my son.

He was battling an insidious and terrible disease.

During the summer of 2014, we took a family trip to Italy; it was the trip of a lifetime. We visited Venice, Florence, Tuscany, Rome, Naples, Pompeii, and the Amalfi coast. It was just the four of us, and I was so thankful we could visit so many beautiful places together.

It was a year after Max was officially diagnosed with depression and a month before his epilepsy diagnosis. Although we have many wonderful memories from this trip, we also have some very difficult ones. It was on that trip Max confessed he'd been unhappy as a child. Bill and I were devastated.

We couldn't understand how and why he felt that way. We reflected upon all the advantages he had, all the privilege he had grown up with, and all the love we had lavished upon him. We honestly couldn't reconcile his feelings with our family as we knew it.

Looking back, I realize it wasn't really Max who was speaking but his illness. He wasn't able to see things the way we would have liked because he was battling an insidious and terrible disease. There were times he described the darkness he felt, and frankly, it was scary.

I can't imagine going through life with that darkness. Life is hard enough—all the tragedies outside of our control that we are powerless to do anything about. I can't fathom how hard it would be to have an inner darkness as well.

As he matured, his perspective from his childhood began to shift. Even though he struggled as a child at times, he realized that our family was special, and he was fortunate in many regards. I'm so thankful he came to this realization. I'm so thankful we had many frank conversations before he passed. I'm so thankful we were able to say many of the things that needed to be said.

In essentials unity, in non-essentials liberty, in all things charity.

Recently, the topic of unity has been at the forefront of my mind. In Christianity, a well-known saying about unity is, "In essentials unity, in non-essentials liberty, in all things charity." Basically, this phrase encourages Christians to be in agreement on core doctrinal issues but to give latitude to secondary ones. This is easier said than done.

As he approached adulthood, one of the issues of faith that Max struggled with was the hypocrisy in the church. Yes, I've heard all the platitudes about the church being for the "sick" and that everybody is hypocritical, but shouldn't we who follow Jesus be different?

So many people are turned off from Christianity by Christians themselves. Often we are self-righteous, legalistic, and judgmental. We are supposed to be a witness for Jesus in a hurt and broken world, yet so often we push others away from Jesus, rather than attracting them to Him.

I don't want to be that kind of Christian, in part to honor Max. He could sniff out hypocrisy like no one else, and he readily called it out. One area of frustration, in particular, was the lack of commitment to justice in the church. As a passionate crusader for justice, he could hardly tolerate it. He was always in support of the underdog, and that's one of the many things I loved so much about him. Perhaps it was because he was often an underdog himself. He struggled, so he fought for other people who struggled as well.

"So many people are turned off from Christianity by Christians themselves. Often we are self-righteous, legalistic, and judgmental."

I want to demonstrate the authenticity and integrity so lacking in our world. I want to share my struggles openly to help others. People need us Christians to be compassionate, loving, kind, and accepting. Just like Jesus was.

"God wants my trust, praise, and worship, but He's big and gracious enough to take the other stuff too."

I believe God can handle anything I throw at Him.

Even before Max passed, I didn't sleep well. I would often wake up in the middle of the night and lie awake for hours. I've continued this sleep pattern in the months since he passed.

Almost like clockwork, I awake at 2:00 or 3:00 am, unable to fall back asleep. I've started to use this time to have conversations with God.

I'm still not doing a good job of praying during the day, but I often have an internal dialogue with Him in the middle of the night. Sometimes I thank Him for my blessings because, despite losing Max, I still have many things for which I'm thankful. Sometimes I silently cry over the loss of my sweet boy. Sometimes I rail against Him for taking Max from me.

I believe God can handle anything I throw at Him. Yes, He wants my trust, praise, and worship, but He's big and gracious enough to take the other stuff too. I'm grateful for His compassion and mercy.

Sharing photographs and memories with others has been a way for me to keep his memory alive.

In October 2019, we lost our sweet family dog, Cookie. I was leaving town for a few days and had arranged for a new dog sitter to watch her. Cookie had been a little under the weather, so I took her to the vet to get her sorted out. While there, they did bloodwork and discovered she was in kidney failure. They recommended we euthanize her immediately, to end her suffering. To say we were shocked and surprised is an understatement. We left the clinic with broken hearts. My eyes were swollen from crying for days. It was all so sudden and unexpected.

A few days later, I went on social media and asked friends and family to share their memories of Cookie. Stories and anecdotes began to flood in and reading them was a tremendous source of comfort. I laughed and cried at all the crazy stories people shared, but ultimately it was a way to keep her memory alive.

The same is true of these reflections I've written about Max. Sharing photographs and memories with others, has been a way for me to continue to talk about him and keep his memory alive. Sometimes, because of a particularly poignant or funny recollection, I forget he's gone.

I read recently about a woman who hoped to live a good life so her loved ones would have a "garment of loving memories to keep them warm" after she'd gone.[19] Max did this for us.

"a 'garment of loving memories to keep them warm' after she'd gone."

Grief is hard. Life is hard.

Sitting on my porch I hear the soft cooing of the Mourning Doves. The Mourning Dove sings a melancholy song, hence its name. While other birds make louder and more raucous noises, the Mourning Dove's soft, sad cooing reminds me of my broken heart.

At times, it's been hard for me to show my emotions since Max passed. I struggle with how and where to do so. After he passed, people warned me I would likely break down at the most inopportune times and places like grocery store lines. I really haven't, though.

I think part of me feels like I have to keep it all together, that I need to present a strong and composed face to the world. Meanwhile, I often feel empty and lifeless inside.

I've said I want to grieve on my own terms, and I truly hope that I'm not stuffing my emotions. I want to process my grief in a productive way, but I'm not always sure what that looks like. This is unchartered territory. Frankly, it's territory I wish I didn't need to travel.

Grief is hard. Life is hard. Sometimes I wonder if I'm doing either one right or if there's even such a thing as doing it "right?" I'm trying.

...try to enjoy the life I've been given.

I recently heard that grief and resilience live together. I'm not sure I understand what that means. Perhaps it means that, although at times I'm overwhelmed and consumed by my grief, resilience is what keeps me going.

There were many times right after Max passed that I honestly didn't care if I lived or died. I struggled to get out of bed, and some days didn't. I wondered if I'd ever enjoy life again.

Despite those feelings of sadness and despair, I kept going. Sometimes, it was for others, like Bill and Sam. Sometimes, it was due to an activity or event. I didn't understand, or even like this resilience at times, but it seemed to be part of me.

"I didn't understand, or even like this resilience at times, but it seemed to be part of me."

As the months pass, there are times I do enjoy life. I know that Max would want this for me. I believe he often felt like a burden to us, and he thought his death would free us. Oh, how wrong he was!

I miss him every day. While I don't miss the worry and fear, I miss his sweet face, his deep voice, and his interesting perspective. There have been many times since he passed that I've thought, "I wonder what Max would say about this?"

One day, I'll be able to ask him these questions. Until then I'll continue to miss my sweet boy and try to enjoy the life I've been given.

"I'm certainly not "over" my grief; I'm just learning how to live through it."

It's hard to reconcile these conflicting emotions.

I've been dreaming about Max for months now. In my early dreams, I would see him in unexpected places and be filled with joy, thinking I'd found him. Recently, I've been having dreams in which he is with us at various functions, but we know what's coming. I try to persuade him to stay with us, but he seems resolved in his determination to end his life. We know it's coming; we just don't know when it will happen, and the apprehension is paralyzing.

Last night, I had another dream where he was with us. As usual, I was attempting to convince him not to leave us. He said, "I won't do that. I don't want to put you through it. I have plans for my future and I want to live." I was filled with tremendous joy!

My therapist has told me that all of my dreams are about me regardless of who else might be in them. Perhaps this new dream is my subconscious telling me I should keep living, that I should enjoy this blessed life I've been given. I know that's what Max would want for me because he loved me. It's just so hard.

I have so many blessings, and yet I miss my sweet boy. Yes, there are times I feel gratitude and happiness, and other times I'm filled with overwhelming sadness and despair. It's hard to reconcile these conflicting emotions.

I long for the day when I will be reunited with my Max. Until then, I'll try to enjoy this blessed life.

I don't understand it, but life does go on.

Today marks ten months since we lost Max. Tomorrow is Easter. As these days approached, I expected to be upset that another month has gone by without him, but I didn't expect to be upset about Easter. We haven't spent Easter together as a family for several years. Many years we celebrated Easter in Naples with my parents during spring break, but it wasn't a holiday filled with traditions. I thought I'd be okay.

Yesterday it hit me that I'm not okay. Perhaps it's because this weekend is the ten-month anniversary AND Easter—two milestones. Regardless, my eyes continue to well up with tears as I think about my beautiful boy.

As I've reflected about all the Easters we spent in Florida, I realize we celebrated differently than when we were at home. We went to Easter Sunday service with my parents at a church that was very different from our beloved home church. Because we were traveling, I didn't bring Easter baskets for Max and Sam. I would usually go to the store in Naples, get them some candy, maybe a small gift, and give it to them in a gift bag. Sometimes we had a traditional Easter dinner, but more often than not we were just anxious to get back out on the beach.

Easter always fell on their spring break from school. We had many years of wonderful spring break trips. Max and Sam always looked forward to seeing their grandparents, and we all loved the sun, the warmth, and the beach. Although it's been seven or eight years since we were all in Florida together, my memories are good and vivid. I now realize that Max's health issues really began in earnest following those years of spring break trips.

Those trips represent a simpler time to me. I'm thankful for the good memories, but it doesn't take away my sadness today. Max will never come to Florida again. We will never celebrate Easter together or any other holiday for that matter. The months and years will continue to march on.

"I miss you, my sweet Max. I hope you and Jesus are eating chocolate bunnies together."

If you had told me that life would go on in the days after losing him, I would have scoffed. How could life go on when we've lost someone so precious? How could I ever again do things that would bring me joy? How could I continue to live with a gaping hole in my heart? I don't understand it, but life does go on. I'm certainly not "over" my grief; I'm just learning how to live through it. I miss you, my sweet Max. I hope you and Jesus are eating chocolate bunnies together in Heaven.

He was one of the most knowledgeable and well-informed people.

When Max was a baby and toddler, we read lots of books. He could sit for hours in my lap snuggling and reading book after book. One of his favorites was titled, *Diggers and Dump Trucks*, by Angela Royston.[20] It was about all kinds of construction equipment, and he was fascinated by it.

At the time, they were building new houses in our neighborhood, so during our daily walks we could often see the equipment we had just read about. Max would sit in his stroller with his sweet, chubby hands resting on the tray and take it all in. He was a thinker even at a young age. He would just watch what was happening around him with his beautiful brown eyes and a serious expression on his sweet face.

That never changed. He was a reader and a deep thinker until the end. He was inquisitive and constantly learning. He was one of the most knowledgeable and well-informed people I knew. It's a shame more people don't share those same qualities.

One of the hardest things is living with the tension between blessings and regrets.

Bill and I have spent the last couple of months in Florida. It's been rejuvenating to escape the cold, gray winter at home. We're so thankful for this beautiful place and our good fortune to be able to spend time here. Yesterday, after Bill and I had a long walk on the beach, we called Sam. He was in a great mood and had lots to report. He's planning to move into a new house in the city with friends, he's dating a darling girl we adore, his job is going well, and he's been climbing and running with friends. Overall, he's thriving.

We hung up the phone, and I was overcome by the blessings in our lives. Then I felt the stab of regret over Max. Max will never do all the things Sam will. He will never move into a new house. He will never again date his beloved Bridget. He will never know the satisfaction of a rewarding and challenging job. He will never participate in the activities that he enjoyed with friends. It just seems so unfair.

One of the hardest things is living with the tension between blessings and regrets. I just read that the hardest part of healing after you've lost someone you love is to recover the *you* that went away with *them*.

I don't know if I'll ever recover the "me" that went away when we lost our sweet Max. I guess acknowledging the profound change is a start. I will forever be different due to losing my son. I will have to learn to live without him, which is in many ways unfathomable. I will need to learn how to feel joy again, with a huge part of my heart missing. A part of me died with Max, and I just hope what's left is big enough to love the people who are left.

A Celebration of Life in Photos

January-March

Max and best friend Joey, age 4
"Those two were inseparable!
They played together almost everyday"

Max, 7 & Sam, 4

"Max quickly adjusted to having a little brother. Sam loved his big brother. Whenever Max was around, Sam would watch him with laser focus and laugh at everything Max did.

As they got older, Max took on his role as Sam's protector. He intervened when he felt Sam was treated unfairly and stood up for him when necessary."

Max, 10 & Sam, 7

Max & his "beautiful head"
12 Months (humpty dumpty)

Max with Cousins at the Beach, 2003

Max & Cookie Evelyn, 2007

"She was a four-and-a-half pound ball of fur... we all fell instantly in love...Her middle name, Evelyn, was Max's idea. He thought since he and Sam had important sounding middle names, she should too."

a beautiful homecoming

APRIL & MAY

Physical pain is preferable to the emotional pain.

I just returned home to Pittsburgh after a couple of months away in Florida. I've begun the task of spring cleanup in my gardens and have been working for hours each day raking, cutting, digging, and dragging tarp after tarp of yard debris into the surrounding woods. At the end of the day, I'm exhausted and sore all over.

As I lay in bed at night, my muscles and joints ache. This physical pain is preferable to the emotional pain of dealing with my loss. It's easier to focus on my physical soreness rather than the mental anguish of losing Max. I'll never again sit with him in my garden. He'll never suggest a new project, like the victory garden he encouraged me to plant last spring. He'll never see the beauty of the pink dogwood tree friends gave us following his passing. It's now planted in the Max Memorial Garden.

Max was proud of our home and gardens. Several years ago, he encouraged me to apply to a Master Gardener program through a local university. Shortly after he passed, a friend of his told me that he loved this property and these woods. I will continue to work to make our property beautiful in his honor.

"I will continue to work to make our property beautiful in his honor."

...little whispers from God that He's still here.

This morning I received an email from a friend. As I scanned the email it appeared to be about a book she was recommending on grief. I replied to her about how hard it is to be back home after spending a couple of months away. This is Max's childhood home, and everywhere I turn, there's a memory.

I told her that when I garden, I think about how Max used to joke that I loved my plants more than I loved him and Sam. I relayed a particularly funny story about a time Max and Sam built a raft for Cookie, our Cairn Terrier, to send her down the raging rapids of a creek after days of rain from a hurricane.

When they told me their idea, I suggested they first "test" the raft with something besides Cookie to make sure it was safe. They returned a while later, white-faced, saying, "Oh Mom, we can't put Cookie on the raft. She'd drown." I shared that this story is both sweet and heart-wrenching.

A few minutes later, my friend responded by telling me that she had forwarded the email because below the book description was an excerpt that recounted how the author lost her son due to a white-water rafting accident. I was blown away! I have a million memories of Max. What are the chances that I would share that particular story with that particular friend? How odd!

Things like that are happening all the time. I guess they're like little whispers from God that He's still here. That he hasn't abandoned me despite my anger and apathy. It's an example of the God Moments I was told to be on the lookout for. Thank you, Lord, for these tiny glimpses of you.

Mental illness is often demonized and criminalized.

Another Black man is dead. Another unarmed man killed by police. The horrors of the past year continue to pile one on top of another. One of my greatest sorrows is that when a Black man is killed by police, people immediately start blaming. People on the right stand staunchly behind law enforcement and blame the victim. People on the left cry for reform, rightfully so, but seem to paint all police officers with the same broad brush of brutality and racism. Why can't we lament the loss of another Black man's life, seek reform of a system that's clearly broken, AND empathize with the job our law enforcement officers are called to do.

I heard recently, that when a 911 call is received about a person having a mental health crisis, the police are sent to the scene. Not paramedics, not therapists, not mental health providers of any kind, just police officers. Police officers are not sufficiently trained or qualified to respond to a mental/behavioral health crisis, and when they are the first responders, the risk of an altercation and/or tragic outcome increases. We are setting our law enforcement officers up for failure in these delicate and frightening situations.

According to a study by the Treatment Advocacy Center, individuals with an untreated mental illness were sixteen times more likely to be killed by police. Since 2015, law enforcement offices have fatally shot more than 1,300 people with mental illness, many of them Black.[21]

Max was an activist, and he lived with a mental illness. He understood better than most that mental illness is often demonized and criminalized. We need a better system to respond to people who are suffering with a mental health crisis. That's not anti-law enforcement, it's simply common sense. I want to help people understand mental illness better, so it's not stigmatized or marginalized.

> *"I want to make my boy proud. I want to make a difference in his honor.*

Max attended marches, rallies, and protests—one just a couple of weeks before he died. I'm so proud of the stands he took. I didn't always agree with them, but I respected and admired his position. He was one person who actually researched issues from different angles and sought out various sources *before* forming an opinion. I want to do the same. Max challenged me to get more involved in important issues when he was alive, and he continues to challenge me since his death. I want to make my boy proud. I want to make a difference in his honor.

"It (love) always protects, always trusts, always hopes, always perseveres. Love never fails."

It's been eleven months since we lost Max. It seems unbelievable that time has continued to march on despite such a profound change in our lives. As the months have passed, memories of Max continue to flood my mind.

One such memory was of a homecoming dance during his freshman year of high school. It was his first dance, and he was excited and asked a girl to go as his date. Max and his friends made plans for pictures, dinner, and a post-dance party. At first, his date told him she couldn't make it for pictures, then she informed him she couldn't make it to the restaurant for dinner, then she told him she would meet him and the rest of their friend group at the dance.

When I went to pick them up after the dance, Max came out to the car alone and dejected. His date was getting another ride home. It turned out she'd ignored him most of the night. Max was so disappointed, and Bill and I were furious.

We laid in bed that night, plotting her murder, or at the very least how to extract from her the money he'd spent on her corsage. I told Bill, "I'm calling her parents tomorrow, telling them what a brat their daughter is and asking for reimbursement for the $25 cost of the corsage." I was in full "Mama-bear mode."

Most parents can relate to this reaction. Hurt my child and you answer to me. It was yet another lesson about my limitations in protecting and sheltering my sweet boy. I simply could not tolerate anyone who didn't appreciate and value him as I did.

I have had my regrets since Max's death, but I believe he never questioned my love for him. He knew I was always on his team. He knew I would do anything for him. I'm forever grateful I have this assurance.

When we parent, we make lots of mistakes. One thing we should never regret though is loving our child. I don't look back and say, "I wish I'd demanded his cooperation and compliance when he was a difficult teenager" or "I wish I'd insisted he pick up his toys when he was young" or "I wish I'd enforced a stricter sleep schedule when he was a baby." It's not that these things aren't important, it's just they aren't most important.

You may have heard, "Good is the enemy of best." While well-behaved, cooperative, and respectful children are good, this shouldn't be the goal of our parenting. Instead, I believe our goal should be to love our children, so they know deep in their bones that our love does not depend upon their performance or personality, but that it's unconditional just like God's. What's most important is love.

One of my favorite passages in Scripture is 1 Corinthians 13. Most people are familiar with the first couple of verses, "Love is patient, love is kind." (13:4), but my favorite verses are, "It (love) always protects, always trusts, always hopes, always perseveres. Love never fails." (13:7-8a) These verses most accurately describe the way I tried to love Max, not always perfectly but unwaveringly and unfailingly. I believe he knew this.

Mental illnesses often begins during adolescence.

In 2007 we made a family mission trip to Costa Rica. It was through the Student Ministries department at our church, so there was a large group of teens as well as a few families with younger children like ours. Max was thirteen at the time and although he was part of the youth group, he was several years younger than most of the other teens. He didn't feel like he fit in with them, nor did he feel like he fit in with the younger kids who were participating with their families. He was in no man's land, and he acted accordingly.

He was incredibly difficult on that trip. He was combative, sarcastic, disrespectful—overall he acted like a sullen teen. I remember being so exasperated with him at one point, I followed him into the men's bathroom to yell at him.

His teen years were hard. He had been such a sweet and compliant little boy, but when he turned thirteen it was like a switch was flipped. I don't know if it was typical adolescent hormones, or due to the early onset of his mental illness, but I often wondered, "What happened to my sweet boy?"

"The issues are typical, but the level of emotion is not."

I remember going with him to get a physical prior to getting his driver's permit and bursting into tears in front of the doctor. The doctor asked what was going on, and I relayed the usual parent and teen difficulties. He responded by saying, "The issues you're facing are typical, but the level of emotion is not." I don't know if that said more about me or Max.

Although mental illnesses can occur at any age, the onset often begins during adolescence. According to the American Psychiatric Association, 50% of mental illnesses present by age 14, and 75% by age 24.[22]

Signs and symptoms can include sleep or appetite changes, mood changes, withdrawal, increased sensitivity, apathy, and other unusual behavior. When these symptoms coincide with puberty, it's often difficult to determine the cause.

Mental illnesses are occurring in our youth more frequently. According to the American Journal of Managed Care (AJMC), "rates of mood disorders and suicide-related outcomes have increased significantly among adolescents and young adults, and the rise of social media may be to blame."[23]

I'm not someone who usually decries the evils of social media, and I think it can provide a platform for positive content. But we do need to be aware of its adverse impact on those most vulnerable, our children and youth. We also need to be on the lookout for behaviors in our children and youth that could indicate any type of mental illness. Mental/emotional health is just as important as physical health, and we all need to start treating it as such.

"Mental health is just as important as physical health."

Smells seem to have a stronger link to memory and emotion than any of the other senses.

Last night sucked. We went through Max's clothes. It took us almost an entire year to work up the courage to do it, and it was even more brutal than I imagined. He had a LOT of clothes. As we went through bag after bag and bin after bin with tears streaming down our faces, we were struck that many of the clothes still smelled like him. Smelling him as we opened up the bags was even worse than the sight of the clothes.

Smell is a funny thing. Smells seem to have a stronger link to memory and emotion than any of the other senses. According to research, scents go directly to the small center of the brain, known as the olfactory bulb. The olfactory bulb is connected to the amygdala and the hippocampus which might explain why the smell of something can so immediately trigger a detailed memory or intense emotion.[24]

Max smoked and seemed to smoke most often when he was stressed. Opening those bags and smelling the cigarette smoke on his clothes brought back the painful memories of all the times we ran to him when he was in crisis.

But mostly the smell of him just made us sad. It made us miss him more. It makes his death more final. Going through his clothes is just one more step in processing and accepting his death. It's another step in the grieving process, and it's one of the most difficult things parents have to do.

I don't feel like a whole mother.

Sunday is Mother's Day, and I've been dreading it. It will be the first Mother's Day without Max. Last Mother's Day was one of the last times we were together as a family, and those memories are still fresh. I've been thinking, "How can I celebrate when I don't feel like a whole mother?"

In the midst of this impending dread, I got together with a sweet friend whom I've known for several years. I met her when she was a freshman in high school when I began to volunteer with our youth group at church, and we've kept in touch throughout her college years. She's a caring, wise, and empathetic young woman. I've always been drawn to her, likely due to her wisdom and compassion.

When she came over the other night, she gave me a Mother's Day card. In it, she wrote, "I know this Mother's Day will be painful. Know that you are an amazing mother and so loved by your sons and many others." Included in the card was a gift certificate for a website that makes commemorative jewelry so I can order something in Max's memory. To say I was moved by her card, kind words, and thoughtful gift is an understatement.

I was not blessed with daughters. Although I love having boys, a part of me always longed for a girl. God has been gracious in sending me several girls and young women who are part of my life. I love them like daughters. I'm incredibly blessed by these relationships. I'm also thankful I didn't or won't have to parent those lovely girls during their tumultuous teen years.

Connecting with these young women over the past year has given me peace and brought joy into my life. They've loved me and supported me, and I'm immensely grateful for these relationships.

My greatest fears is that he will be forgotten.

Max was a quirky card giver. Is that even a thing? He was known for giving Hanukkah cards for birthdays, get-well cards for anniversaries, and graduations cards for Mother's Day. It was all part of his schtick. His thank-you notes were entertaining as well. He used to say, "If I have to write thank-you notes, I may as well have a little fun."

Sam is continuing the tradition. He gave Bill a birthday card last night with an illustration on the front of a girl in a glittery dress and big hat that read, "Best year ever." It was ironic in more ways than one.

"I will continue to help others to remember and get to know him."

We're all trying to honor Max in our own way since he passed. We all want to stay connected to him and keep his memory alive. I feel this deeply. One of my greatest fears is that he will be forgotten, and I can't allow that to happen. I will continue to help others to remember and/or get to know him because he truly was the most interesting person I've ever known.

I pray God helps me focus just on the day in front of me.

I was talking to my therapist about the approaching year anniversary of Max's passing. During our conversation, she told me that the second year is often actually worse. Worse? How is that even possible?

She stated that the first year is a year of firsts: first holidays, first birthdays, first Mother's Day…all without him. The second year is the beginning of forever. This reality hit me like a ton of bricks!

I told her, "I don't know if I can handle that!" to which she responded, "You didn't think you could handle this past year either, and yet, here you are." I'm so incredibly thankful for her wisdom and insight.

I really can't imagine how next year will be harder. This past year has been the most difficult of my life. How can I possibly survive anything worse? The thought is almost unbearable.

A couple of phrases come to mind as I contemplate this future, this forever, without my precious Max: one day at a time and through God's grace. I can't look too far ahead or else I become overwhelmed. I pray God helps me focus just on the day in front of me. Join me in this prayer, please.

"The second year is the beginning of forever. This reality hit me like a ton of bricks!"

I occupy a space that actually frightens other parents, especially mothers.

It's 5:00 am and I can't sleep. Yesterday was Mother's Day. My first Mother's Day without Max. It was awful.

A few years ago, he was hospitalized on Mother's Day. I remember sitting in church that morning weeping and thinking, "How can I celebrate today without my precious Max with me?" If only I had known what was coming.

A friend sent me an article titled, "Mother's Day is for Grieving Mothers."[24] She lost her son a few years ago and knew it would be a particularly painful day for me. There's a line in it that reads, "Today, Mother's Day honors mothers of living children and it should also honor mothers of dead children." It's hard for me to know how to feel without the presence of the person who first made me a mother. I feel like I'm not whole. It's my first Mother's Day without him but only the first of many. However will I cope?

I heard from several people and received heartfelt messages recognizing the difficulty of the day. I also saw and spoke to family members who didn't even acknowledge my loss.

> *"I also saw and spoke to family members who didn't even acknowledge my loss."*

I am angry, disappointed, and discouraged, but I think the emotion I feel most acutely is loneliness. I feel like I occupy a space nobody else can understand. I feel like I occupy a space that actually frightens other parents, especially mothers. I feel like I occupy a space some people are too self-absorbed to even acknowledge. I feel overwhelmingly alone. Perhaps things will look less grim when the sun comes up. Until then I'm feeling lonely and sorry for myself. I miss my Max.

Promise and potential that is lost.

Yesterday we celebrated Michael's graduation from medical school. Michael is my sister, Kelly, and brother-in-law, Rocco's son. He was Max's closest cousin. They were born only four months apart and were fast friends from a very young age.

When they were together, they were in a world of their own. They always had lots to say to each other, and it was hard to break into their conversations. They were both intelligent and well-informed. It was fun to simply listen in on their banter.

Michael grew up in York, Pennsylvania, and came to Pittsburgh for medical school four years ago. He fulfilled his lifelong dream to live here with his bestie cousin.

Yesterday was bittersweet. We are so proud of Michael and his achievements, and yet Max's absence was crushing. He would have been so proud of Michael. He loved Michael and admired him greatly. Michael has a bright future ahead of him, and Max would have been his biggest cheerleader along the way.

Yesterday also reminded us of all Max won't accomplish now. That's been one of the hardest things to reconcile—all of Max's promise and potential that is lost.

I told Michael yesterday that I'm sure Max is looking down on him and smiling. I just wish my sweet boy could be here smiling in person. He had the most amazing smile.

A Celebration of Life in Photos

April & May

Mother's Day, 2020

"Know that you are an amazing mother and so loved by your sons and many others."
[words from a friend, one year later, Mother's Day 2021]

Max, Freshman Year, Homecoming

Max & Michael, 1995

Max & Michael, both 13, 2007

"I told Michael yesterday that I'm sure Max is looking down on him and smiling. I just wish my sweet boy could be here smiling in person. He had the most amazing smile."

Costa Rica Mission Trip, 2007

JUNE & JULY

This grief journey is not linear.

A friend reminded me of a memory from this time last year. Max and his roommate were looking for a third roommate at their house, so Max had posted pictures and a description of the house on social media. Reading his words and hearing his voice in my mind was incredibly hard.

Looking back, I believe he was getting things in order. I don't know how long his plan to end his life was in place, and frankly, I can't even think about it.

As the anniversary of his passing approaches on June 3rd, I'm filled with so many swirling feelings. I feel like a bowl full of emotions and when I get "bumped" something sloshes out. Sometimes it's sorrow, but other times it's anger, irritation, frustration, or resentment.

When I'm around people complaining about things I see as inconsequential, I find myself wanting to scream! And if I'm honest EVERYTHING seems inconsequential to losing a child. I know it's not a contest, but I can't help to compare.

I'm realizing this grief journey is not linear. I honestly thought I would move through the commonly accepted five stages of grief: denial, anger, bargaining, depression, and acceptance in that order. I thought once I experienced one, I would be done with it and move on to the next. I was wrong. I've found myself circling back to each stage again and again.

And let's talk about acceptance. What does acceptance of Max's death even look like? I don't believe it's some sort of miraculous peace that will come upon me allowing me to live "happily ever after." There is no happily ever after when you've experienced such a profound loss.

Maybe acceptance looks more like learning to live with a part of me missing, like learning to walk again after losing a leg, only it's my heart that's been severed.

"What does acceptance of his death even look like? Maybe acceptance looks more like learning to live with a part of me missing."

As I've shared my feelings and reflections over the past year on social media, many people have told me how helpful they've been. Most of these people haven't lost a child, but they have experienced a loss. Even though loss is universal, the way each of us deals with our loss is unique and individual. Don't fall into the trap I did thinking you should be further along or through a specific stage by a certain time. Give yourself the time and space to fully grieve with no expectations, and definitely don't allow the expectations of others to dictate your grief process. Grieving is intensely uncomfortable, but necessary, and having people walk alongside you through the process is invaluable.

I can honestly say I could not have endured the last year without the love, support, and encouragement of my family and many friends. I'm forever grateful.

I'm barely keeping my head above water.

As the anniversary of Max's death approaches, I'm filled with a sense of impending doom. Dread isn't exactly the right word. We dread going to the dentist. We dread an upcoming test or presentation. Looking towards the anniversary of my son's death is so much more than that.

Impending doom is feeling something tragic is going to happen. Something tragic has already happened. We lost our Max a year ago.

My therapist told me what I'm feeling is due to my body and my mind getting ready for the anniversary of his death. According to her and other experts, our bodies remember this type of trauma at a cellular level. I'm not sure I understand that. All I know is that I'm struggling. We're all struggling.

It's so interesting how differently Max's death has affected us and how we're each approaching the anniversary. Bill is anxious and controlling. Sam is stressed and overwhelmed. I'm apathetic and angry.

I guess that's because we're not just dealing with the death of a loved one, we're dealing with trauma. Both trauma and death require processing and healing. Perhaps that's why we all seem to be falling apart as the anniversary approaches.

"I'm struggling to deal with my own emotions, and I can't take on any more."

I've been feeling like I'm barely keeping my head above water. As I watch Bill and Sam struggle, it makes me feel like I'm about to go under. It's not that I don't care how they're feeling. Of course, I want to know, so I can love and support them. It's just that I'm struggling to deal with my own emotions, and I can't take on any more. June 3rd will arrive in a couple of days. I hope we all make it through.

Worry and hope have been replaced with sorrow and despair.

The last photograph we have of Max is from my mom's 82nd drive-by birthday party last year. It was Sunday, May 24th, and we had gathered at my mom's senior living facility to celebrate with her. COVID restrictions were in full force, so we had set up a table outdoors with cupcakes, sparkling wine, and balloons. Friends and family drove by and honked and waved. Some people stopped and got out of their cars to wish her a happy birthday. It was certainly a different type of birthday party.

In the photo, Max and Sam are standing behind my mom wearing masks I had made for them and their sunglasses. Their expressions are hidden and unreadable.

After leaving my mom, Max, Sam, Bill, and I got a pizza and sat together at a nearby park. We talked and laughed as we usually did when together. Sam had just graduated from college without any sort of ceremony or fanfare and was lamenting looking for a job during a pandemic. Max suggested he spend the night at his house so they could hang out and talk. It was the last time we saw him alive. He died eleven days later.

When I look at this picture, lots of memories come flooding back. I remember the close and loving relationship Max and Sam shared. I remember how Max always looked out for his little brother. I remember Max's fierce loyalty to family. I also remember all the struggles my sweet boy had to endure. I remember all the crises and setbacks. I remember the gut-wrenching worry I lived with for years. I can still feel the physical effects of that worry when I think about it, things like a roiling stomach, shallow breathing, and racing thoughts.

As difficult as that worry was to live with, living with his death is even harder. While he was alive, there was hope. Hope that he would eventually get better. Hope that he would continue to take better care of himself. Hope for a better future.

Now, worry and hope have been replaced with sorrow and despair. I have to cling to the assurance that he is in Heaven with Jesus otherwise I simply couldn't survive.

A couple of friends recently encouraged me to read and study more about Heaven. They suggested it will give me peace now and hope for the day when I will be reunited with my Max. I know Heaven is better than here. I know Max is in a better place, as cliche as that sounds, but this life is all I know. I'm still living in this world. As comforting as it should be to think of my precious boy in the loving arms of Jesus, I still wish he were in mine.

"As comforting as it should be to think of my precious boy in the loving arms of Jesus, I still wish he were in mine."

Perhaps this is more specific to women and moms in particular. We're so accustomed to putting the needs of others ahead of our own that we lose sight of our own desires and needs.

Since Max's death, I've been a little more willing to put my needs first. Perhaps part of it is that I simply don't have the emotional bandwidth to deal with everybody else's junk. I have enough of my own.

Grief makes us selfish because we're so wrapped up in our own pain.

My therapist recently introduced me to the idea that many of us operate in a FOG. FOG is an acronym for Fear, Obligation, and Guilt. She stated that most of what we do on a daily basis is because we're afraid of what others will think of us, or an obligation versus a desire to do something, or from a position of guilt. I don't know about you, but this resonates deeply with me.

I think grief makes us selfish because we're so wrapped up in our own pain, and it's hard to recognize or care about the pain of others. I hope I don't live in this state forever. I hope that my loss makes me a more compassionate and loving person. I also hope that once I'm a bit more stable, I have the courage to work through my issues, so I don't walk around in a FOG.

I want to be the kind of wife, mother, sister, daughter, and friend who does things out of love, desire, and honor, NOT fear, obligation, and guilt. Perhaps with God's grace and lots more therapy I'll get there.

Grief is just love with no place to go.

It's June 3rd—a full year since we lost our precious Max. In many ways, it's hard to believe we have endured what has been the most painful year of our lives. I wasn't sure we would.

Yesterday I received a letter from a friend who lost her son several years ago. She shared many things she learned during that first year. It resonated deeply with me. Just a few include:

"I learned about real, deep, prolonged sadness. How sadness can really take your breath away, how it can feel like it's crushing your chest and obviously your will and spirit."

"I learned that 'being on' and functioning when your heart is broken is exhausting. It's really hard to act like you're okay."

"I learned that I have more friends than I thought and that there are a whole lot of people who care about us."

I, too, learned these and many other lessons this past year. Frankly, they're lessons I wish I didn't have to learn.

As I look towards the future, a future without Max, I recognize that nothing will ever be the same. A day won't go by that I don't think about him. A day won't go by that I don't miss him with every fiber of my being. A day won't go by that I don't wish things had turned out differently.

I recently found a picture from Max's first birthday. When I look at his sweet chubby face, I'm reminded of all my hopes and dreams for him and

"I learned that 'being on' and functioning when your heart is broken is exhausting. It's really hard to act like you're okay."

my deep, all-encompassing love. I'm so thankful I didn't know then what was coming. If I'd known I would only have him for such a short time, I would have been paralyzed with fear. I would have smothered him in my efforts to keep him safe.

I do know I loved and will continue to love my boy fiercely. My love will never die even though he has. I've heard grief is just love with no place to go. I will wait expectantly for the day I can once again love my precious Max face to face. Until then I will look for ways to honor his memory and legacy because that's something tangible I can do with the overwhelming love I have for him.

Getting the tattoo was worth the pain to have a permanent, visual reminder of my precious Max.

This past Saturday, we got tattoos in memory of Max. Bill's tattoo is of angel wings with the inscription "My sweet Max" below. Sam's tattoo is a rendering of a badass photograph of Max from the Pittsburgh protest in May of 2020. Mine is the bottom half of the Jesus Saves sketch Max drew for me a couple of years ago. Instead of "Jesus Saves" written in the banner, mine reads "My beloved Max" and the font is in his handwriting.

We all selected different tattoos with a special meaning for each of us. We had them done by Max's very talented tattoo artist. Getting the tattoo hurt like heck, but it was worth the pain to have a permanent, visual reminder of my precious Max. I got mine on the inside of my right ankle. I picked this place because I wanted to be able to see it myself and easily show it to others. Bill and Sam got their tattoos on their upper arms for the same reason.

Max had seventeen tattoos himself. Each one had special meaning to him. I didn't understand them at the time, but I do now. I want to tell people the meaning behind my tattoo, and I think he did too. Tattoos can be a special way to express yourself and to share who and what is important to you. No one is more important to me than my family.

"No one is more important to me than my family."

A friend suggested that Max watched us get our tattoos on Saturday and cheered us on from Heaven. I hope this is true. I hope he knows we gladly endured the physical discomfort in our desire to honor and memorialize him. I hope he knows how much we love and miss him. I hope he knows how important he is to us.

Perhaps artists are able to see below a surface and superficial smile.

We have received many thoughtful gifts since Max passed. We just recently received two more that really touched me.

The first is a blanket made from his clothes, mostly t-shirts. As we unfolded it and noted all the different shirts, I could picture Max wearing them. Many were band t-shirts that he purchased at the concerts and shows he attended over the years. He loved music and loved wearing t-shirts of his favorite bands.

This blanket is soft and cozy, and I look forward to wrapping myself up in it someday but not today. It's too hard. Those memories are too raw. I will use the blanket eventually, and I'll cherish it for as long as I have it. I just need a little more time before I'm ready to use it.

The second gift was a painting of Max, done by a friend. I began to cry the minute I saw it. Our friend captured Max's smile and expression so beautifully. He made the painting from a photograph of Max, taken about nine months before he passed. I remember taking that photo of him at a time when he was on an upswing. He looks happy and content. He was at an event with people he loved.

continued on next page

We have many pictures of Max where I can see the pain in his eyes even though he's smiling. Perhaps our friend used this particular photo for that reason. One where Max looks at ease. Perhaps artists are able to see below a surface and superficial smile. Regardless, I'm thankful for this painting of our beloved Max.

I just pray at some point the joys outweigh the sorrows.

Today is Father's Day. It will be a day when many post beautiful pictures on social media of days spent with family, and in the past, I would have done the same. I would have posted pictures of Bill with Max and Sam from over the years and written about what a loving, supportive, and engaged dad he is and always has been. I would have wished him a very happy Father's Day as we prepared to spend the day together as a family. That won't happen again this year.

Neither Bill nor I remember Father's Day from last year. We were clearly in shock. Today will be an especially hard day for Bill, as he has to celebrate once again without the person who first made him a dad. This year the absence of our sweet Max is particularly hard.

Bill and Sam will go golfing and enjoy their time together, but it just won't be the same. It's these special occasions that are so difficult—days we will never celebrate with Max again. And I worry about the pressure we may be inadvertently putting on Sam to be and do all the things we wished for both our boys. After a year, I now know the loss doesn't get any easier. I just pray at some point the joys outweigh the sorrows.

I've been overcome with regret, sadness, and anger about a beautiful life that ended too soon.

I've read several books on grief, and they often recommend making an effort to remember the good times. Particularly if someone was very ill and suffering before their death, negative flashbacks and disturbing memories can come flooding back and can be exhausting.

What I remember, has moved through different stages since Max died. At first, I was relieved that his suffering and our worry were over. After the shock and that initial relief passed, I was overcome with memories that pointed to his promise and potential, which will not be realized now.

Rather than looking back with fondness and gratitude for the time we had with him, I've been overcome with regret, sadness, and anger about a beautiful life that ended too soon.

I hope I can get to the point where I can reminisce in a positive way, where I can think about him and truly be thankful for his life rather than being filled with sorrow and despair.

Is that too much to ask? Can I ever achieve that level of peace and acceptance? I don't know. Honestly, from where I sit, it seems unfathomable. One of my grief books is filled with short prayers that often resonate with me. One about memories is this, "Lord, renew my strength and refresh my mind with peaceful, happy memories." Can it happen? If so, only the Lord can do it.[26]

I think when tragedy strikes, a mother's natural response is to gather her children close.

Sam moved out yesterday. He will be living in a beautiful house in the city with several friends. He's looking forward to being on his own after living at home this past year.

I, on the other hand, am less excited. He moved back home last summer immediately following Max's death. We didn't ask him to, but we were incredibly relieved when he did. Providentially, he also got a job locally that allowed him to stay in Pittsburgh. It was a comfort to have him home. I think when tragedy strikes, a mother's natural response is to gather her children close.

Even though Sam's been living with us, he was rarely at home. Between his work, friends, activities, and our travels, we've been lucky to see him for a few minutes each day. Over the winter, we went several months without seeing him because of our time in Florida.

For all these reasons, I'm surprised by how greatly his move is impacting me. Lately, he's been struggling with the anniversary of his brother's death and about his future. Frankly, his struggles have been a trigger for me—they've brought back memories of Max and all of his struggles.

All of this has caused me to worry and want to keep Sam close. Even though I didn't see him every day, I KNEW I could if I wanted. Just having him home was a comfort. Now I won't be able to lay my eyes on him daily and it scares me.

I just read a quote that struck me. "Sometimes in grief, you will cling too tightly to family members who are still living because you fear losing them as well."[27] I can relate, and I fear that's what I've done with Sam.

"Sometimes in grief, you will cling too tightly to family members who are still living..."

I think Sam moving out is probably what's best for him. He will be surrounded by friends and living in a vibrant part of the city. He's focused on caring for himself as he deals with the ongoing struggle of losing his brother. I think it's best for him, I just don't know yet if it's best for me.

I hope to regain patience and truly feel compassion for people who are struggling in any way.

I had a conversation recently with someone who has experienced more than her share of tragedy in her life. She was telling me that although it's been difficult to deal with these situations, all her experiences have made her a more compassionate and understanding person. She looked at me and stated knowingly, "You probably feel the same." At the time, I simply nodded my head but all the while I was thinking, "Hell, no!"

I really WANT to become a more compassionate and understanding person, but I'm not there yet. I'm still so angry about Max's death. *continued on next page*

Over the last several months, I've heard of other families who have lost a child to suicide. Yes, I've felt compassion for these unfortunate families. I've reached out when appropriate to express my condolences and support; however, to say I'm generally more compassionate and understanding is a gross overstatement.

"There's just so much nonsense in this world, and my tolerance for it is drastically diminished."

Frankly, I don't know if I'll ever get there. There's just so much nonsense in this world, and my tolerance for it is drastically diminished. In the future, I hope to regain patience and truly feel compassion for people who are struggling in any way. For right now though, I'll just try to get through the day without losing it.

Reality has fully set in.

I recently read an article about depression, titled, "Seven Subtle Signs of Depression You Shouldn't Ignore."[28] The seven signs are:

1. Irritability - got it
2. Sleep difficulties - got 'em
3. Aches and Pains - got 'em
4. Decreased energy - got it
5. Feelings of guilt - got 'em
6. Reckless behavior - got it
7. Concentration problems - got 'em

My therapist keeps telling me I'm depressed. I'm taking medication. I'm in therapy. It's been a year since we lost Max. I don't feel any better. As a matter of fact, I feel worse now than I did right after he died. Reality has fully set in.

People tell you that time heals. People say grief diminishes over time. People say eventually I'll feel normal again. None of that has happened yet and I'm not sure it ever will.

The second year is harder than the first.

As I've read over my journal entries from the past year, I'm struck that they've gotten less hopeful as time has gone on. At first, I expressed relief that my sweet boy was no longer suffering. I truly believed he was in a better place, as cliche as that sounds. I expressed assurance that he was in Heaven with Jesus. I expressed hope that one day I would be reunited with him. I still think and believe those things, but they bring me far less comfort now than they did months ago.

Perhaps at the beginning, I was in such intense pain, I thought, "Surely this can't last." I was wrong. The pain has continued and in some ways has intensified because all the shock and denial have worn off.

Now I'm left with the reality that I have to live the rest of my life without my Max and it's excruciating. Over and over again, people keep telling me the second year is harder than the first. Although this is our reality, our loss has faded in the eyes of others. It's not that our support system has abandoned us, but life goes on. The first year is over. Max's death is not the focus for others that it is for us. That's another thing that makes the second year so hard. I hope to feel hopeful at some point. I hope my hope returns. Until then, I just miss my son.

I can cry just as readily as I can scream.

Luke 6:45 reads, "What you say flows from what's in your heart." The meaning is that if your heart holds joy, love and contentment, you will express these qualities in your speech. If your heart is full of bitterness, anger, and sorrow, these too will be expressed in your speech. I'm in trouble.

I'm often surprised by what comes out of my mouth. I've started to use words I haven't used before. I'm easily irritated and quick to express it. A friend recently observed that my rage seems close to the surface.

Frankly, I think all my emotions are closer to the surface than they used to be. I can cry just as readily as I can scream. I find my eyes are constantly welling up with tears. Is this normal? I have no idea. I've never navigated this kind of pain and grief before. I've never been a year out from the loss of my son and wondered why things aren't any better now.

I was recently with a young mom and her new baby. She's in the stage where she's completely in love with him. She doesn't just love him, she's IN LOVE with him. If you've ever had a baby, you'll understand this feeling. Just looking at him is overwhelming. She said she holds him while he sleeps and marvels at his perfection.

"If you've ever had a baby, you'll understand this feeling."

I felt that way about Max and Sam, but Max was my first. I remember being completely overcome by my love for him. I remember thinking he was the most beautiful baby I'd ever seen, and I was shocked that Bill and I had created him.

I guess this overwhelming love is why my heart is so twisted up in knots now. I guess this love is why my words have become more negative and profane than at any other time in my life. I think eventually, the love I feel for Max will have a more positive outlet; until then I think everyone can deal with a little swearing.

Blessed is the one who perseveres under trial.

JAMES 1:12 NIV

Several years ago, I memorized the book of James from the Bible. I was in a bible study where the teacher encouraged us to write out the entire book and memorize it. I've always loved this particular book because it's filled with practical advice for living, so I accepted the challenge. It's a relatively short book, only five chapters, so memorizing it wasn't as difficult as I anticipated. It also helped that I was familiar with and appreciated the content.

I haven't recited the entire book in a couple of years, but I'm thankful certain segments frequently come to my mind to help me understand or navigate something I'm dealing with.

continued on next page

"Humble yourself before the Lord and He will lift you up."
- James 4:10 NIV

Many books on grief quote Bible verses from the book of James. Verses like the following have spoken to me over the past year:

"If any of you lacks wisdom, you should ask God, who gives generously without finding fault." - James 1:5 NIV

"Blessed is the one who perseveres under trial because, having stood the test, that person will receive the crown of life that the Lord has promised to those who love him." - James 1:12 NIV

"Come near to God, and He will come near to you."
- James 4:8a NIV

"Humble yourself before the Lord and He will lift you up."
- James 4:10 NIV

"Therefore confess your sins to each other and pray for each other so that you may be healed. The prayer of a righteous person is powerful and effective." - James 5:16 NIV

I continue to appreciate the wisdom and advice in this book. I pray it continues to provide comfort and peace in the days ahead. I'm thankful every time a nugget from it pops into my head.

I feel as if I'm barely here.

Since Max passed away, I've connected with several other moms who have lost children. I'm thankful for these connections because nobody understands the loss of a child better than a mother who has lost one.

Most of these women have echoed my thought that one of the hardest parts of losing a child is loneliness. It's hard to put into words just how lonely this journey has been. Although our network of family and friends has been incredibly supportive and compassionate, none of them can truly understand what we're experiencing.

I recently watched the movie, *A Little Chaos.*[29] In one scene, a group of women gathered and began to discuss the loved ones they had lost. It was set in the seventeenth century, so many spoke of losing children. They talked openly about how they had lost their children, many to disease and others to accident. I guess during that time period it was much more common to lose a child, and every woman in the group discussed losing one or more of her children.

Perhaps that's why it feels so lonely to lose a child in our time. It's simply not as common. The women in previous time periods understood from personal experience how profoundly losing a child impacts a mother. Perhaps there was a bit of comfort at that time in knowing they were not alone.

During this scene in the movie, one of the characters was an older woman who had lost all her children and her husband. As she was sharing her story and her feelings, she lamented, "I'm barely here."

I can relate to this sentiment. In some ways, I feel as if I'm barely here too. I don't know if this feeling will fade over time or whether I will feel this way until I die. I do know most people can't understand my feelings and that makes the loneliness harder to bear.

I have anger and aggression to work out.

I took a boxing class last week. Several months ago, my therapist recommended I try boxing as a way to release my anger and frustration. She suggested that hitting things would be healing and therapeutic.

Max was into boxing. Actually, he was into Muay Thai which is Thai kickboxing. In the last year of his life, he had joined a Muay Thai gym and was taking several classes a week. He not only enjoyed Muay Thai for the intense workout, but I think he also benefited from the release of frustration and aggression he got from hitting and kicking things. In his personal items, he left two sets of boxing gloves.

During my boxing class, I used one set of his gloves. As I was putting them on, I was filled with conflicting emotions. I felt close to him, placing my hands inside gloves he had worn many times. I also felt intense sadness that I was using them instead of him. I was overcome with the thought that he should still be here enjoying his Muay Thai classes.

"I felt close to him, placing my hands inside gloves he had worn many times."

I'm going to try and incorporate boxing into my routine. Lord knows I have anger and aggression to work out. And by boxing regularly, I can feel closer to my sweet son.

June & July

Bill's Tattoo

Sam's Tattoo

Erin's Tattoo

"A friend suggested that Max watched us get our tattoos... and cheered us on from Heaven. I hope this is true. I hope he knows we gladly endured the physical discomfort in our desire to honor and memorialize him. I hope he knows how much we love and miss him. I hope he knows how important he is to us."

Bill & Max, 1997

Grandma's Birthday, 2020

"When I look at this picture, memories come flooding back: the close and loving relationship Max and Sam shared, Max's loyalty to family, and all of his crises and setbacks."

Max's 1st Birthday, 1995

"...his sweet chubby face, reminds me of all my hopes and dreams for him.."

AUGUST THROUGH OCTOBER

You do not need a great faith,
but faith in a great God.

As an avid reader of historical fiction, I've read many books over the years about WWII. One of the things I've found most puzzling in my reading is the accounts of the vast number of people all over Europe who lost their faith in God as a result of the war. I've often thought, "Why on earth would someone make it through such a horrific ordeal only to lose their faith? Couldn't they see God's protection and provision as they looked back?" Yes, many people endured unspeakable tragedies, but I've always thought their tragedies should have made them more thankful, more resolute, and stronger in their faith.

That's what I thought before this last year. That's what I thought before we experienced the horrific loss of our Max.

Over the years while he was sick, my faith remained strong and steadfast. I believed in a God who can and does heal people. I believed in a God who answers prayers. I believed in a God who has authority over all things. I honestly thought He would answer my prayers to heal Max, and I thought that healing would occur while my sweet boy was still living.

Yes, God did heal Max. Max is no longer in pain. He's no longer suffering. He is free from the illness and struggles he faced in this life. Yes, I believe that, but I still feel distant and aloof from God.

What makes my doubts, and at times my ambivalence, even harder to handle is that I don't THINK I should feel this way. In my head, I can say God was and is still with us. I can say, He's never left our side. I can say, Jesus understands my pain better than anyone because He experienced the most intense pain ever. My head can believe those things, but my heart is a different story.

In my grief, I still can't reconcile the loss of my precious boy. I can't understand why he is gone. I can't fathom how this could be the outcome of his life. Although I don't believe God caused his illness and subsequent death, I can't for the life of me understand why He didn't stop it.

"Although I don't believe God caused his illness & subsequent death, I can't understand why He didn't stop it."

I hope I get past this anger, doubt, and ambivalence. Truth be told, I thought I would be past it by now. I fully expected to feel at least a little better by now.

There seems to be a constant battle between my head and my heart. I know things in my head that I don't feel in my heart, not even a little bit. I hope this changes. I hope this tragedy doesn't cause me to lose my faith like so many others who have experienced a profound loss. I hope my faith is strong and steadfast enough to endure. I have heard the following quote, "You do not need a great faith, but faith in a great God." (James Hudson Taylor) I guess I need to rely on that truth.

The "strain" of this life got to him.

I read the following quote in a book recently, "Strain. It gets even the best brains. Sometimes the best brains are the ones it gets the worst."[30] This was true of Max. He used to joke that it would have been easier to be stupid. He hypothesized that perhaps people who aren't as intelligent are oblivious to the many injustices and problems of this world. Perhaps their lack of awareness prevents them from processing all the evils of our world. Perhaps this ignorance is protective. Perhaps ignorance really is bliss.

When Max joked in this manner, I would tell him, "That's not a very nice thing to say," particularly if he was talking about a specific person, but I understood his meaning.

My Max had one of the "best brains" I've ever known. I guess in some ways it was one of the best and in some ways one of the worst. He was highly intelligent, but also suffered from two brain disorders, depression, and epilepsy. What I do know is that the "strain" of this life got to him the "worst," and that reality makes me profoundly sad. I'm thankful his "best brain" is finally at peace.

I cannot imagine going through the loss of a child without faith.

I recently heard about a mother who tragically lost her young adult son this past spring. Of course, she's distraught and devastated. It's unfathomable to lose a child suddenly and tragically.

She is asking all the questions we asked after losing Max. "Why him? Why is our family forced to deal with this? How can we go on without him? What does life without him even look like?" I understand all of these questions, but some she's asking are hard for me to grasp. She's asking, "Is there a Heaven? Is there even a God?"

I cannot imagine going through the loss of a child without faith. I cannot imagine the despair a mother would feel if she truly thought this life is all there is, and that she would never again see her precious son.

The past year has been brutal, and I do have faith. I've struggled with hopelessness and despair, but I've also been assured time and time again that Max is with Jesus and one day I will be reunited with him. Through my anger, doubt, and ambivalence, I still believe these promises. If I didn't believe them, I don't think I could go on. What would be the point? If I truly thought I would never see my precious Max again, my heart would shrivel up and die.

I hope this woman is just going through a crisis of faith. I understand that, but I sincerely pray she rediscovers Jesus.

Self-pity comes much more naturally than gratitude.

I recently spent time with a person who has a victim mentality. She laments that others get what she wants and what she deserves. She feels that other people and circumstances are to blame for her problems. She believes bad things will continue to happen to her. She wallows in negativity and isn't much fun to be around.

As she talked, I kept thinking, "Why don't you focus on the good in your life? Why don't you focus on what you have rather than what you don't have?" Then it struck me, I've become just like her.

Since losing Max, I've become so fixated on his death that I've lost sight of my many blessings. It turns out self-pity comes much more naturally than gratitude. They say grief makes you noble. Nonsense! I don't know who came up with that idea, but it's simply not true in my experience. Grief makes you selfish and hateful. The jealous and unkind thoughts I've had over the last year are embarrassing.

I can recall specific times in my life when I've been overwhelmed with gratitude. Times I've been so overcome with my blessings that I've literally been brought to tears. I haven't felt that way in a long time. I guess admitting you have a problem is half the battle. I sure hope I can get over my anger and self-pity and begin to see my blessings again. I hope I can begin to practice gratitude because lots of practice is what it will take for me to feel grateful once again.

"I hope I can pretend to practice gratitude because lots of practice is what it will take..."

He's using this tremendous potential in Heaven.

This week, I took Talysha and Ny'airah to Kidzone, the day camp at our church. Talysha is our goddaughter, and Ny'airah is her cousin. It was fun, albeit exhausting, to have them spend the week with us, and to take them to the same day camp their uncle Rafael attended with Max and Sam.

Max was six years old the first time he attended Kidzone. He attended as a camper until the 6th grade and then served as a teen leader throughout high school.

It was bittersweet to take the girls this week. It brought back all the memories of the boys attending when they were the same age. Max was an attentive and well-behaved camper. The campers were broken up into small groups of about ten kids by age and gender. There were always several very active boys in Max's small groups, so he was typically a favorite among his leaders for his calm demeanor.

Each day when I picked up the boys from camp, Max was the only one able to recount the Bible story they'd learned and share with me the application they had discussed. I would joke that perhaps he would one day be a pastor.

I had so many dreams for him. He was full of promise and potential. When I look at pictures of him from his Kidzone days, I see a sweet, sensitive, and thoughtful boy with an uncanny understanding of faith in God. To think that this sweet boy would become so sick and feel so desperate when he got older is too much for my heart to handle. I feel like his amazing potential was wasted. Hopefully, he's using this tremendous potential in Heaven.

The fact that we couldn't protect or save him is heartbreaking.

I've been struggling to understand why I've felt so sad and desperate these last few weeks. The anniversary of Max's death is past us. All the "firsts" I dreaded over the last year are over. I know I've said it before, but I really expected to feel a little more normal by this point.

I was doing some research on grief recently and it turns out the loss of a child is the worst because it's frequently called "the ultimate tragedy."[31] This article listed common responses to a child's death that include:

- Shock
- Denial
- Replay
- Yearning
- Confusion
- Guilt
- Powerlessness
- Anger
- Loss of hope

I have experienced every single one. As I read through my journaling from the past year, I can see these responses reflected again and again.

The ones that have been especially difficult and surprising are replay, yearning, powerlessness, and loss of hope.

The number of times I've replayed the day of Max's death are too many to count. I've pondered every "what if" I could possibly entertain.

The yearning I've felt over the past year goes way beyond the mental and emotional—it has impacted me physically, too. I've felt a profound physical yearning for him—to hug him, to kiss him, to talk with him just one more time. I've heard that parents who lose a child often develop physical ailments from the stress and grief of their child's death. I'm frankly surprised this hasn't happened to me.

For me, the powerlessness and loss of hope go hand in hand. I felt powerless and hopeless at times while he was still alive, but those feelings have increased a hundredfold since his death.

To face the fact that we couldn't protect or save him is heartbreaking. To face all the milestones he won't achieve takes my breath away. This article acknowledges that parents experience an upsurge of grief when faced with these milestones, oftentimes in the lives of your child's peers. I can relate.

My therapist keeps telling me the second year is the hardest. Some suggest that I can expect to experience profound and intense grief for at least eighteen months. I simply don't know if I can make it. I'm not sure I want to.

"...the loss of a child is the worst because it's frequently called "the ultimate tragedy."

Mention the deceased by name.

In the book *Through a Season of Grief*, there is a list of suggestions for how to interact and communicate with someone experiencing grief.[32] Several from the list include:

- Mention the deceased by name.
- Do not say that you know how they feel. Each loss is different.
- Let them cry and express their emotions.
- Don't change the subject to a lighter topic for your own comfort.
- Do not tell them how good they look to avoid talking about how bad they feel.

It's interesting to reflect on how people over the last year have modeled, or not modeled these suggestions.

Recently, I saw a woman whom I haven't seen in several months. As we were talking, she exclaimed several times, "You look great!" It was as if she was surprised by my appearance, but I now see it as a defense mechanism. She most likely didn't want to talk about how I'm actually feeling.

During our conversation, my eyes welled with tears which is a very common occurrence these days, and I could tell she was uncomfortable. She made promises to call me so we could get together, but I knew she just wanted to get away. I don't blame her. I know it's wildly uncomfortable for many people to be around us because we've experienced every parent's worst nightmare. We're a walking reminder of the horror that can befall a family.

On the other hand, we have friends who have walked beside us throughout the last year and given us the latitude to say, feel, and look whatever or however we want. We are blessed beyond measure to have them.

It's a wonder, literally, that you've helped to create such a perfect and beautiful little person.

When Max was young, strangers would often comment, "He's beautiful." I would respond with wonder in my voice, "I know!"

My mom used to laugh and tell me that I was supposed to respond with "Thank you." But I would reply, "They didn't compliment me. They were complimenting him and I'm simply agreeing." I think most moms can relate to being awed by the beauty of their children. It's a wonder, literally, that you've helped to create such a perfect and beautiful little person.

When Max was a baby, he got lots of attention when out in public. He was adorable. He had a large, round, bald head that many people admired and commented on. One time we were in a store, and a woman commented, "I've been admiring his big ole, round, pumpkin head." Perhaps some parents might have been offended by this comment, but not me. I, too, appreciated his big, beautiful head.

Other people remarked about his expressive, huge brown eyes. His eyes continued to be expressive throughout his life. I could tell how he was feeling just by looking into his eyes.

Since he's passed, I've posted many pictures of him throughout his life on social media. The most common response I've gotten has been, "What a beautiful boy!" He was a beautiful boy with beautiful eyes and a beautiful heart. All I can say is, "I know!"

"I could tell how he was feeling just by looking into his eyes."

A giant wave was crashing over me and threatening to keep me under.

One of the things I've struggled with over the last couple of months is that I really don't feel any better. As the anniversary of Max's death came and went, I felt like a giant wave was crashing over me and threatening to keep me under. I've commented frequently over the last few weeks that I feel like I'm barely keeping my head above water.

Just in the last few days, I'm beginning to see the water recede. I'm trying to reframe my thoughts. I'm realizing it does no good to assign arbitrary dates like, "I should feel better by ______." Grief doesn't work that way. Grieving the loss of a child definitely doesn't work that way. Grieving the loss of a child doesn't follow any specific timeline or guidelines.

I think, instead of focusing on getting to a "better" place, I should just focus on getting to a more manageable place. That's probably a good strategy. "Better" is still a long way off. I just need to settle for "manageable".

"'Better' is still a long way off."

What gets suppressed, gets expressed.

Distraction has been a technique I've employed throughout my life. If something has been uncomfortable or too painful to face, I've found it easy to find other ways to occupy my time and my mind. That way I don't have to face or think about the things I don't want to. I've done this quite often over the last year. Actually, Bill and I both have. We've kept ourselves busy with project after project.

Distraction was a technique we utilized in parenting as well. When Max and Sam were little, we often used distraction to keep them from crying or prevent them from doing something we didn't want them to do. We used to think, "Let's pick our battles." If distraction was effective, we thought, "Why not?" It prevented altercations over every little thing.

Distraction serves a purpose, but it can't be the only tool we utilize. I recently heard, "What gets suppressed, gets expressed." I love a pithy phrase, so it stuck. It also stuck because it's true.

I need to process my emotions. If I ignore or suppress them for too long they come out in unhealthy and unproductive ways. I think this is why it's so easy for me to get angry and irritated. If I'm not dealing with my feelings, they come out sideways. In other words, they get "expressed" in a way that isn't particularly helpful for me or beneficial for others.

That's why writing these reflections has been so helpful. They've helped me process what I'm feeling and put into words the swirling emotions I've experienced since losing Max. It also feels productive. Rather than just sitting with my emotions, I feel like I'm expressing them in a healthy way.

I have a feeling I'll continue to try to distract myself, but hopefully, I can balance busyness with other healthy coping strategies.

Grief IS complicated.

These past two days have been some of the hardest since losing Max because Bill picked up his ashes from the funeral home. It took us more than a year to do so. It's been something that we've known we had to do but just couldn't summon the courage.

I was driving home the other day, thinking, "Is this my life now—just sadness and sorrow?"

I'm continuing to research grief and came across yet another set of stages of grief: shock, sadness, anger, guilt, acceptance, and hope. I think it makes sense there is a stage after acceptance, namely hope. I've struggled thinking about what acceptance might look like. Is it just acknowledgment that he's gone? Does acceptance indicate I've moved on in my life? Does it mean I'm no longer as sad?

If I think about it as simply acknowledging he's gone, then it makes a bit of sense. I don't like it. I wish it were different, but it's the reality. From there perhaps I can move towards hope, namely hope for the future. Hope that eventually, the intense pain will subside. Hope that I'll be optimistic about my life again. Hope that my life will have meaning and purpose as it once did.

In my research, I've come across the term "complicated grief" which is defined as a persistent complex bereavement disorder where the feelings of loss are debilitating and don't improve over time.[33] Complicated grief typically occurs more frequently in older females. Risk factors include an unexpected or violent death (such as suicide) and the death of a child.

I asked my therapist if she thought I had complicated grief to which she responded, "Grief IS complicated." Yes, it is! It doesn't help that I've not been down this road before. I didn't know what to expect, what's normal, or if there is a normal. What I do know is that I continue to be surprised by how intense and long-lasting my grief has been. Grief is hard, messy, unpredictable, and complicated. I don't know if anyone experiences a simple grief, but I know I sure haven't.

"I don't know if anyone experiences a simple grief, but I know I sure haven't."

It's validating to hear people echo my feelings and thoughts.

Bill, Sam, and I participated in an online, suicide survivors support group last night. Sam has participated for the last several weeks and suggested that Bill and I do the same. I was reluctant at first because I didn't want to infringe on Sam's space, but he assured us that other families participated together. Although he didn't specifically mention that he wanted us to participate with him, his invitation may have been a clue.

The facilitator seems to be a lovely man who has been leading groups for thirty-four years. That kind of compassion and commitment is incredibly unusual and special, and he lives in Naples, Florida of all places.

We joined the meeting along with twenty-eight other participants of various ages from all over the country. Many had lost children but others their spouses, fiancés, parents, and friends. Each story is heartbreaking. Yet it was oddly comforting to see those faces and hear their stories. It's validating to hear people echo my feelings and thoughts since Max died.

continued on next page

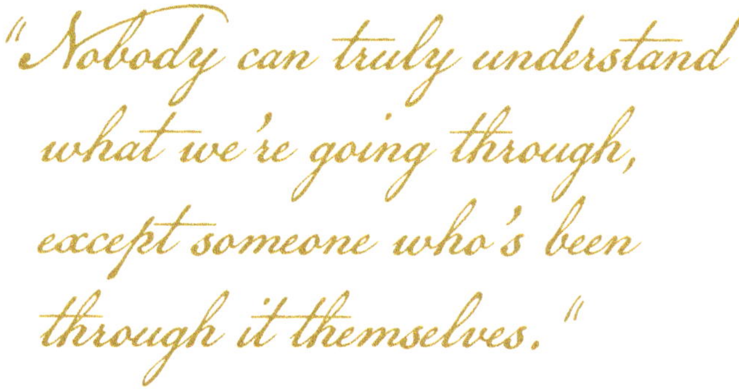

The facilitator and several long-time members of the group told us that we'd come to the right place for healing and comfort. Nobody can truly understand what we're going through, except someone who's been through it themselves. I'm hoping that, through participation in this group, I'll feel less lonely because I will be surrounded by people who understand. I'm hoping I can process my anger. I'm hoping I can get to a place of actual optimism and hope for my future.

I don't know why it took us more than a year to join a support group. Many of the people who spoke last night, lost their loved ones much more recently than us. One woman was only four weeks out from her loss. I suppose there's a time and a season for all things. It's possible we needed the first year to process on our own the best we could. After all, we have a fantastic support system, but few can truly relate to our pain. I hope this group of strangers will become our friends and a vital part of our healing and support system going forward.

Why do so many view mental illness as a weakness, a mood, a passing phase, or perhaps worst of all a behavioral problem?

Since Max passed, I've read several books written by authors who have lost someone to suicide. The most recent was *His Bright Light, The Story of Nick Traina*, by Danielle Steel. [34] Unlike her better-known romance novels, this was the true story of her son, Nick, who died in 1997 at the age of nineteen as a result of his bipolar illness.

Reading about her son was in some ways like reading about Max. He was extremely bright, an early talker and reader, suffered from sleep disturbances and was exceptionally creative and sensitive. Like Max, her son was a musician who performed in several bands including a hardcore punk rock band. Music was a huge part of her son's life, just like it was for Max, probably, in part, because music speaks to people on an emotional and spiritual level.

Danielle Steel describes how Nick often changed his hair color and/or style and continued to get tattoos throughout his life. Max did the same. It was a way to express himself, but I also believe he felt so bad on the inside that he thought it would make him feel better if he changed something on the outside. My sweet boy had no idea he was perfect just the way he was.

This wasn't the first book I've read that describes what seems to be a prototype of a person suffering from mental illness. The similarities among them are staggering.

In the prologue, Danielle Steel writes, "This is the story of an extraordinary boy with a brilliant mind, a heart of gold, and a tortured soul." Yep, that describes my Max too. She goes on to write, "His illness killed him as surely as if it had been cancer." When describing bipolar she writes, "You have to understand what you're dealing with, to accept that what you're dealing with is the equivalent of not just a bellyache, but liver cancer." Yep and yep.

"You have to understand what you're dealing with, to accept that what you're dealing with is the equivalent of not just a bellyache, but liver cancer."

Danielle Steel shares the belief that one-third of those diagnosed with bipolar will die from it, possibly as many as two-thirds. This is because statistics are somewhat soft on fatalities that may be attributed to other causes, rather than suicide specifically. These are terrifying statistics. Something needs to be done.

Why do so many view mental illness as a weakness, a mood, a passing phase, or perhaps worst of all a behavioral problem? When are we going to realize that mental illness is every bit as serious as physical illness?

There are estimates that suicide is the second leading cause of death among individuals between ten and thirty-four, and according to the Center for Disease and Control, the suicide rate in persons aged ten to twenty-four increased 56% between 2007 and 2017. Suicide is an epidemic.[35]

We have a serious problem, and we need to solve it. I believe the first steps are awareness, education, and more comprehensive mental health care. There's lots of talk about eradicating cancer or other diseases by pouring more time and money into research. Are we putting the same resources into researching mental illness? I don't think so, but we should.

Not all grief is equal.

Random, out-of-order, life-altering loss. That is a phrase I just came across in a new book titled, *It's Okay That You're Not Okay*, by Megan Devine[36] The author is a psychologist who watched her partner die tragically and unexpectedly. She realized after this experience that her previous counseling of patients who were experiencing grief was lacking, and much of our corporate understanding and expectations of grief are flawed.

First, she makes the case that "random, out-of-order, life-altering losses" are the hardest to deal with. Death is never easy to deal with, but when it's out of the blue (random) and out-of-order (losing someone before their time) it contributes significantly to being "life-altering."

People like to equalize grief by saying things like, "It's never easy to lose someone you love." While this may be true, not all grief is equal. It's probably easier to lose a parent than a child. It's easier to lose an elderly person rather than a young person. It may be easier to lose someone who has been sick for a long time

continued on next page

rather than someone who dies suddenly. By telling people that all grief is equal, we tell them that the devastation they're feeling may be invalid.

In this book, the author explains why certain comments are less than helpful. Comments like:

At least you had him for as long as you did...

He's in a better place now...

You have so much to be thankful for...

He's no longer suffering…

You're stronger than you think…

Everything happens for a reason…

We've heard these and countless other well-intended but unhelpful comments since Max passed. These comments hurt because there is a second, unsaid part to them. The unsaid piece is really something like, "So stop feeling so sad" or "Snap out of it" or "How long are you going to wallow?"

If someone were to actually say, "Everything happens for a reason so snap out of your sadness. I mean, honestly, how long are you going to grieve?" we would all consider that person a monster. However, that's often the unspoken meaning behind the comments people frequently make to those who have lost a loved one. I understand, I really do. When someone else is wracked with grief, it's so tempting to try to make sense of the loss or to say anything that comes to mind to try and make them less sad.

Because our culture treats grief like a problem to be solved or something to "get over, so much grief support is unhelpful. Rather than fixing someone's grief, what if we just came alongside them? What if we simply acknowledged their feelings rather than try to "solve their problem?"

We need to stop looking for meaning in meaningless things. The reality is that I may never find meaning in Max's death. I do hope to use my experience of losing him in some productive way, but that doesn't mean his death was "meaningful."

> *"Rather than fixing someone's grief, what if we just came alongside them?"*

The author makes the point that in our culture we are obsessed with happy endings and redemptive stories. It's a tall order to have a happy ending or to find redemption when dealing with the death of a beloved child.

I will never get to the point where I believe losing Max has made me a better person or in some way has made my life better. Never. Let's stop being so fixated on silver linings. Silver linings don't always exist and telling those who are grieving that they do is unhelpful and unkind.

Terrible things happen suddenly and randomly to people, all the time.

Another comment many people make to us is, "I can't imagine." I think what they really mean is they don't WANT to imagine because it's far too painful and scary. When someone suffers a catastrophic loss, it's human nature to try to do whatever we can to distance ourselves from their situation. Admitting there are things in life that are random and unpredictable and can destroy our lives in the blink of an eye is just too much for most of us to handle.

I understand this. It's much easier to operate under the illusion of control, believing that the tragedy that has befallen someone else could never happen to us. In reality, though, terrible things happen suddenly and randomly to people, all the time.

Those "I can't imagine" people also frequently convey it through their actions and body language. Some are so wildly uncomfortable around me that I find myself comforting them. I find myself reassuring them with comments like, "We're lucky we have a strong support system. We're lucky to have faith. God is giving us the strength to get through every day." Does this strike you as crazy as it does me? It speaks to the warped perception many people have of the control they have over their lives.

I appreciate friends who simply say, "I'm sorry." I appreciate when they don't feel like they need to say anything more to acknowledge my thoughts and feelings or try to make sense of our tragedy. I appreciate the people who support and encourage *me* rather than the other way around.

> *"Admitting there are things in life that are random and unpredictable and can destroy our lives in the blink of an eye is just too much for most of us to handle."*

It's like being buffeted by waves in the ocean.

The other day we went down to Max's house to inspect and clean after a tenant moved out. While we were there, we collected a stack of mail that was delivered to him in the months since his death. Being at the house where he lived for two years, was hard, and going through his mail was even more difficult.

Included in the stack of mail were notifications of canceled insurance policies, closed bank accounts, and other vivid reminders of the finality of his death. The worst piece of mail, though, was an invoice from an EMS company from the day of his death.

Believe it or not, this company mailed an invoice for transporting his body to the morgue. It was addressed to Maxwell Blechman, not "next of kin." Is that really a common occurrence, to invoice a deceased person? It was like the cruelest of jokes.

There have been many things over the last fourteen months that have taken my breath away, but this was one of the worst. I honestly couldn't believe it, and for the life of me, can't explain it. I thought for one nanosecond about calling the EMS company, but just decided to throw the invoice in the trash.

Even though I discarded it, I can't discard the memory. The cruelty and injustice of such a thing is stunning.

Since he passed, I continue to be caught off guard by things I didn't expect or couldn't anticipate. It's like being buffeted by waves in the ocean. Just when one recedes, another slams into me. There have been times I've wondered if one of these waves is going to keep me under, and other times I've wished one would.

I don't know how many more of these waves I can expect, or how long they will continue to crash into me, but I can only hope and pray they will lessen over time.

"I continue to be caught off guard by things I didn't expect or couldn't anticipate."

My grief won't fade or diminish because my love for Max will never fade or diminish.

I'm sitting here with a box containing Max's ashes. Later today we will hold a small, private ceremony and place his ashes in his memorial garden. Both Bill and I have written letters we hope to read during the ceremony assuming we can make it through them without completely breaking down.

As I sat down to write my letter, I realized that over the last fourteen months I've literally written thousands of words, although very few, if any, have been written directly to Max. It's been easier for me to write stories about him and record my experiences over the last year rather than writing to him.

It's hard to believe this box contains what was once his body. I loved his body more than my own. It was a body I carried in my own. It was a body I tenderly and lovingly held and bathed and fed and kissed and changed and hugged and so much more. I know his soul and essence left this earth last June, but I still want to honor his body through this ceremony because I love him so much.

As he grew up, his body was so full of life and beauty. It's hard to believe it's been reduced to this small box.

In many ways, I still can't believe he's gone. I wonder if he knows how hard losing him has been for all of us. I wonder if he knows all the pain and tears his death has caused.

One thing I've learned is that because I loved him so deeply, my grief has been intense and at times debilitating. I honestly thought my grief would fade or diminish at least a little by this point. Don't we hear that time heals all wounds? Nonsense. Some wounds are simply too deep to ever heal. I now know that my grief won't fade or diminish because my love for Max will never fade or diminish. I will long for him and miss him until the day I die.

"I honestly thought my grief would fade or diminish at least a little by this point. Don't we hear that time heals all wounds? Nonsense."

People have told us this ceremony is an important step in our healing. They tell us it will give us a sense of closure we haven't yet had. I now understand the wisdom of the traditions related to death. I now understand that burying a person's body shortly after death gives the family much-needed closure. The decision over what to do with his ashes has been hanging over our heads for the past year. I am hopeful that finally putting him to rest will provide a bit of peace and closure. I'm hoping that placing his ashes in his memorial garden will help me feel like he's close to me. I hope to receive some comfort from sitting in his garden and talking to him.

I don't know. This is another new and gut-wrenching first, and in some ways, I'm just looking forward to putting it behind me. It's just another time I need to say goodbye to my beloved son and it's awful. Goodbye, my love. You may be gone but you will forever live in my heart.

It's hard to be the surviving child. We grieve for our sibling and also for our mom and dad.

I recently heard from an acquaintance who has been following my grief journey over the past year. She reached out to share a tragically similar experience in her family. She lost a sibling at a young age. She didn't get into specifics, but she shared how difficult it was for her to watch her parents grieve the loss of their child.

She wrote about her experience, saying, "It's hard to be the surviving child. We grieve for our sibling and also for our mom and dad." As I read those words, fear gripped my heart.

I've often wondered since losing Max how it's impacting Sam differently than me. I've asked him how he is doing periodically, and we've discussed how he's processing it, but I can't really know what he's thinking.

A friend of mine recently observed how he watches me when we're together. It's as if he is carefully gauging my behavior so as to know how to best respond. I find this both incredibly sweet and troubling.

continued on next page

I don't want him to feel like he has to handle me with kid gloves. I don't want him to feel the added burden of dealing with the loss of his brother AND worrying about me. But then again, I worry about him.

Perhaps that's just part of being a family, part of love. We don't just think about ourselves, but we also consider how a tragic life event like this impacts our loved ones.

Over the years, I've had conversations with Sam about how Max's health issues impacted him. He always responded by saying something like, "It's not about me, Mom. I just want to support/help/encourage Max." Now that Max is gone, I feel as if, oftentimes, Sam is more concerned with me than himself.

Yes, he's taken productive steps to deal with his grief, like therapy and the support group. I just hope and pray he doesn't feel the added burden of having to deal with my grief too.

Letting go of our children as they grow up is hard. Letting go of a child who dies is even harder.

Therapy has been a lifesaver over the last fourteen months. Bill and I had a session with our marriage counselor the other day, during which I was explaining how horrific it's been for me to lose Max. I said to our therapist, "Max was my world!"

I was fortunate to be a stay-at-home mom for the majority of Max and Sam's younger years. I worked part-time off and on but parenting and running our household was my primary job, and I took that role seriously. I read books and attended seminars on parenting. I was heavily involved in volunteering at their schools. I prioritized being at home when they returned from school at the end of the day. I prided myself on being an available and engaged mom.

I think it's for all these reasons that Max's death has made me feel like a failure as a mother. Our marriage therapist pointed out that most of my purpose came from parenting. I got most of my value and worth from being a mom. He went on to observe that Bill had and still has a successful, professional career that gives him a sense of purpose and fulfillment, something I don't have.

Even though Max and Sam were out of the house and Bill and I were technically empty nesters, it didn't change the fact that most of my identity was wrapped up in being a mother.

During our therapy session, Bill turned to me and asked, "If Max had died of cancer, would you feel like a failure?" At the time I answered, "No," but upon further reflection, perhaps I would. Do we ever truly believe we did everything we could have done for our children? Don't we all think we could have, should have, or might have done more? Don't most parents mistakenly take responsibility for things that are actually outside of their control?

Why do we do this? Is it merely instinctual parenting behavior? Maybe it's just because we feel responsible for the safety and well-being of our children from the day they're born. Parenting is a job that never ends.

I remember attending a parenting seminar years ago, where I was part of the team involved in running it. An older gentleman was in the kitchen of our church with me as I was preparing coffee and snacks. He asked, "What's going on?" I answered, "We're having a parenting seminar," to which he replied, "Oh, we're all done with that." I remember at the time exclaiming, "We're never done with parenting!" How right I was! Even though Max and Sam were young at the time, I already grasped that my role as mom would continue even as they became adults.

Letting go of our children as they grow up is hard. Letting go of a child who dies is even harder. I pray these feelings of failure lessen over time. I KNOW in my head that I did everything I knew to do with Max, I just hope in time my heart catches up.

Complaining leads to self-pity and rage.

Yesterday I got a call from the new tenant at Max's house. He informed me that he was moving out because he felt uncomfortable living there after hearing about Max's death. He stated, "After hearing the story, I'm uncomfortable and I think the house might be haunted. I feel lied to and deceived." I didn't respond negatively at the time, but after thinking about his insensitive comments, I became enraged.

What kind of person says something so thoughtless to the mother of a son who has died by suicide? He was clearly implying that Max's spirit is haunting the house. How superstitious and absurd!

After ruminating on this conversation for a while, I proceeded to tell the story to everyone I saw for the rest of the day. As I recounted the story my sense of righteous indignation grew. What is it about complaining that feels so good? Is it because it allows us to justify our emotions?

"What is it about complaining that feels so good?"

I heard recently that complaining leads to self-pity and rage, and I can relate. Yesterday as I continued to reflect on this conversation, my anger grew, and my feelings of self-pity became magnified. I already feel tremendous anger. I already feel incredibly sorry for myself. The last thing I need is to add fuel to the fire of these emotions.

These comments were indeed insensitive and unkind, but I allowed them to hijack the rest of my day. I turned over my power and agency to this inconsiderate and immature young man.

When I'm around others who complain, I'm often impatient and judgmental, thinking, "Well, complaining isn't going to change the situation." If this is how I think, why am I so tempted to complain myself? I guess that by complaining I'm trying to garner support for my feelings in order to justify them.

I'd like to try and reframe these negative thoughts. Yesterday I attempted to do this a bit. As I felt my anxiety rising, I tried a minute of deep breathing. I offered a short simple prayer. I tried to focus on the good things in my life. None of these things came naturally. I had to consciously think about doing them. I'd like to get to a place where coping strategies like these become second nature. I'm just not there yet. Hopefully, I'll get there someday.

Just take one day at a time.

A few weeks ago, at church, I observed a young mother with her baby. At first I thought she was pregnant since she had her infant wrapped tightly against her body. All through the service she bounced him and rubbed his head and bottom. Towards the end of the service, she took him out of the baby wrap carrier and handed him to his father sitting beside her.

continued on next page

I watched as he looked up at his mother with a sweet adoring look on his face, and immediately a memory of Max looking at me in the exact same way came rushing back. I felt like I'd been kicked in the stomach. It's situations like this that literally make it difficult to breathe. When something like this happens, it's so unexpected, so out of the blue, I find myself overcome with emotion.

I guess it comes down to expectations. I have enough emotional energy to get through the day as I anticipate it. I make my list of things I have to do, commitments I may have, and then brace myself to get through it all. When something unexpected happens, my emotions can quickly overwhelm me.

I don't think about the future since getting through today takes everything I've got. I don't get excited about good things that may happen in the future because it's hard to imagine that things could actually be good. I guess I should heed conventional wisdom and just take one day at a time. That seems to be about all I can handle.

Each night I can remember, I'm "one day closer."

I keep hearing the phrase, "One day closer." This phrase is used by people who have lost a loved one. Rather than counting the days/weeks/months since they left us, we can end each day by focusing on the fact that we're one day closer to being with our beloved.

The first time I heard it I thought it was rather morbid, but I've changed my mind. This type of thinking actually puts a more positive spin on our loss. Instead of being consumed by the time Max has been gone, I can think about the joy I will feel when I'm reunited with him.

In the book, *Heaven is for Real*, by Todd Burpo, Colton Burpo shares stories with his parents of his visits to Heaven after surviving an emergency appendectomy at the age of four. He tells his parents about the sister he met in Heaven. His sister was never born due to a miscarriage before Colton was born and he knew nothing about her. As Colton assured his parents that his sister was okay, he stated, "She can't wait for you (and Daddy) to get to heaven."[37]

"I can think about the joy I will feel when I'm reunited with him."

What a beautiful sentiment! The idea that Max is in Heaven anxiously awaiting my arrival is both touching and heart-wrenching. I feel the same way. I want to enjoy the many blessings I have in this life AND I can't wait to see and hold and hug and kiss my sweet Max again. Until that time comes, each night I can remember, I'm "One day closer."

I will never be the person I was before my precious boy died.

In the fifteen months since Max passed, I have grieved in a public way. I've posted many of these reflections on social media and have gotten lots of feedback. Some people have been surprised and a bit taken aback by my raw transparency, while others have encouraged me to continue sharing. I've heard many times over the months how helpful my posts have been to others who have experienced a loss.

It's interesting, though, that as time has gone on, I tend to get fewer comments and reactions. I understand this, I really do. How many times can you tell a person how sorry you are for their loss? How many different responses and reactions can I expect from essentially the same group of people? For others, life goes on. I know they are sorry for the tragedy we have suffered, but at this point, it's old news.

Everybody told us to expect lots of comfort, condolences, and support at first, but to understand that after a short time it begins to wane. It's not that people don't care, it's just that everyone assumes time will work its healing magic.

"Everyone assumes time will work its healing magic."

Nobody can truly understand, unless they've lost a child, that this type of loss changes a person forever. I will never "get over" my loss. I will never live another day without this hole in my heart. I will never forget what has happened. The loss of Max is with me every minute of every day.

People keep telling me that my times of sadness will decrease, and times of joy will increase, but it's hard to imagine. I need to accept that I will never "get back to normal." I will never be the person I was before my precious boy died. My new normal is being created every day that I live without my beloved Max. I don't know what it will look like, but I hope I have the strength to continue to put one foot in front of the other until I figure it out.

Grief doesn't just impact a person emotionally and mentally but physically as well.

When I look into the mirror, I almost don't recognize the face staring back at me. I feel like I've aged ten years in the span of one. I see deeper lines etched on my face and pain reflected in my eyes. Turns out grief doesn't just impact a person emotionally and mentally but physically as well.

In a book I just finished, one of the characters talks about this. After losing all of her sons in war, she states, "It is grief which has left its mark on me, not time."[38]

During this past year, my heart has literally ached, my stomach clenched when something unexpectedly reminds me of Max. At night, my mind and sometimes my heart race. And the fatigue! Many days it takes all of my energy to get out of bed and make it through the day. Not having experienced profound grief like this before, these physical sensations have left me feeling surprised on many occasions.

I believe some of these physical responses will diminish over time, but others will have lasting and long-term effects. Such is life, right? The years we live, leave their mark on us. Happiness leaves laugh lines on our faces, while sorrow leaves frown lines and a deeply furrowed brow. I hope at the end of my life I'm fortunate enough to have an equal combination of both.

I'm trying to talk to him.

The other night, at our Suicide Survivors support group, the conversation revolved around talking to our loved one. Many people reported having daily conversations with the person they've lost. Most also described the apparent signs from their loved one in the midst of these conversations. One man described how two hummingbirds hovered nearby while he was sprinkling his son's ashes in the mountains. He assumed they represented his son, so he told them, "I'll be sitting on the deck down at the house later if you'd like to join me." Later as he was sitting on his deck, these same two hummingbirds returned and hovered inches from his face for several minutes. He felt as if he'd been blessed with a visit from his lost son.

After hearing his story, I confessed to the group that I haven't been talking to Max. I literally can't talk to him without completely breaking down, so I've avoided conversation. One of the participants encouraged me to simply say, "Hey Max" right then and there. I was barely able to choke the words out through my tears, but afterward, I felt relief and release.

"I was barely able to choke the words out through my tears, but afterward, I felt relief and release."

Perhaps it was her encouragement or the kudos I got from the group for my effort, but I'm trying to talk to him. When I see his picture, I say, "Good morning, my love" or "How are you today, lovey?" or "Goodnight, my sweet." It's not much, but it's a start. Maybe if I can work my way up to longer conversations, I'll experience some of the signs of him that other group members report. I could surely use a visit from my son. I miss him so much.

Mental illness is much less understood and tolerated than physical conditions we can readily see.

I was recently speaking with a woman who suffers from autism. She had some very interesting things to say about navigating life with her disability. She claims that society is much less comfortable with women who in her words, "act autistic" than with autistic men. Perhaps this is because, by and large, women are more relational than men, and it's those very relational situations that are problematic for someone with autism.

She also shared that people will sometimes say to her, "I would never guess you are autistic! You seem so normal." Although these people mean well, their comments are still hurtful. What's "normal" anyway? Who gets to judge what is normal or abnormal behavior? Comments like this further prove that hidden conditions, like autism and mental illness, are much less understood and tolerated than physical conditions we can readily see. Would anyone ever comment to a person in a wheelchair, "I can't believe you're in a wheelchair! You seem so normal?"

Another observation she made is that people with autism are typically very sensitive. Oftentimes we think of sensitivity to sensory stimuli like lights and sounds, but she said it tends to go deeper and manifest as an emotional sensitivity. She stated that across the board, sensitive people have a difficult time setting boundaries.

I found this very interesting and although she didn't elaborate, I found myself wondering why? Is it that they simply don't know how? If they learned the skills, would they be able to establish and maintain boundaries? Or are their hearts simply too tender?

"Sensitive people have a difficult time setting boundaries."

I found myself thinking about Max as she was speaking. He, too, was very sensitive. He also had a very difficult time setting boundaries, so he let the troubles and pain around him into his mind and his heart. How very difficult it must be to live like this in our broken and chaotic world. Imagine the emotional and mental pain of absorbing all the suffering, injustices, and evils of this world.

Healthy boundaries are essential in self-care because they allow us to say NO to things and not take everything on. Healthy boundaries lead to high self-esteem and self-respect. On the other hand, poor boundaries can lead to hurt, anger, burnout, and feeling powerless.

I see that many of Max's struggles resulted from poor boundaries. My sweet boy was just too sensitive, his heart was too tender for this world, and I'm so sorry for the pain he endured while he was here.

Our family feels so much smaller now.

Last night we attended the wedding of dear family friends. Our kids grew up together and Max was close to their daughter, the bride. The two of them got into some serious antics in their younger years, such as the time they dared each other to eat worms. She was very capable at a young age, Max not so much. One time Max confessed to her that he didn't know how to make toast. She scoffed and scolded, "Max, you put a piece of bread in the toaster and push a button!" They had a sweet, funny relationship.

The wedding was lovely. It took place in a botanical garden, so the setting was absolutely gorgeous. The bride was glowing as she married the love of her life. The reception was full of people we've known for almost thirty years. It was bittersweet.

I knew the day would be difficult. While we are so happy for them, we're also feeling sorry for ourselves. Max won't get married. We won't be able to celebrate the welcoming of a new person into our family. We won't be able to see Max and his potential spouse experience all the joys of marriage and parenthood. I won't get to cry at his wedding as I'm certain I would have done. Releasing him to another woman in marriage can't even compare to releasing him in death.

Our family feels so much smaller now. We didn't just lose Max, but we also lost his future wife and children. It's a compounded loss. Is it selfish to feel sorry for myself? Am I making it all about me rather than simply celebrating a milestone day with our friends? Is it possible to do both? It's living in the tension of celebrating with others and mourning what will never be for us. It's hard. I wonder if it will ever get any easier.

"It's celebrating with others and mourning what will never be."

Doing the things he enjoyed is a way for me to feel like he's still around.

We attended two Pittsburgh Pirate games this summer. Max was a huge fan, so it felt important to go to a game in his honor. Loving the Pirates as he did, can be a fairly frustrating endeavor. Other than a few years here and there, they usually aren't very good. Max often lamented their low payroll—one of the lowest in Major League Baseball—and the decisions made by management about personnel. Nevertheless, he remained a faithful fan listening to most games, even preseason, and tracking team stats.

Other than baseball, Max didn't have much of an interest in sports as he got older. I don't know if it was the nostalgia of baseball or the fact that he considered it a thinking man's sport, but he loved his Pirates! He confessed once that he started to follow the Pirates several years ago so he and Bill would have something in common. Bill is an avid fan of ALL sports. I think Max liked having a common shared passion. A couple of years ago, he gave Bill a sketch he had done, commemorating the 1960 World Series during which the Pirates beat Bill's childhood team, the Baltimore Orioles.

Every summer for the last few years, we would attend a game as a family. I didn't usually enjoy going to the games, truth be told. I found them a bit boring, honestly. So, I was pleasantly surprised this summer over the enjoyment I got from watching the Pirates play.

We had beautiful weather both times, and the Pirates won both games during an overall losing season. It felt good to cheer them on to victory because Max would have been excited to do the same.

Things like this make me feel close to him. Doing the things he enjoyed is a way for me to feel like he's still around. Actually, I believe he was around for both those games. He was with us, drinking a beer and watching his beloved Pirates win. It might sound silly, but I'm attributing the beautiful weather and victories to Max. I like to think he told God, "Hey my parents are there. Let's make it enjoyable for them."

"This precious gift has taken on greater meaning and significance since he passed."

Thanks for being my best friend and my favorite woman alive. I love you, Max

When Max was in high school, he gave me a picture frame one Christmas on which he wrote, "To my beautiful, wonderful, mother, thanks for always listening, for being sweet to my crazy friends, for dealing with me, Sam and Dad. Thanks for being my best friend and my favorite woman alive. I love you - Max"

This gift was all the more meaningful because things were particularly difficult during that time. Max was full of teenage angst and most likely experiencing both depression and anxiety symptoms. He and Bill were butting heads, and I often felt like I was in the middle playing referee.

I appreciated this precious gift at the time, but it's taken on even greater meaning and significance since he passed. It's a gift I will treasure for the rest of my life. Not only is the message he wrote a reflection of his true feelings, but it's written in his actual handwriting.

Max's handwriting was unique. It was messy and at times hard to decipher. He had an interesting habit of forming his letters from the bottom up rather than the top down. I don't know if this contributed to the messiness or not. All I know is when I look at this picture, I see not only a photo of him and me, but I see his sweet words written in his unique handwriting. I'm so thankful for wonderful reminders like this of my precious son.

I sometimes feel so overwhelmed I can't breathe.

Today is Max's birthday, our second without him. I had a busy day planned because I thought if I kept myself busy and distracted, I'd be okay. I was wrong. Max would be turning twenty-seven today. He SHOULD be turning twenty-seven today. The fact that he's not here is so unfair, I could scream.

I woke up last night and couldn't get back to sleep because I was remembering the day he was born. He was two weeks overdue, so I had gone into the hospital the night before. They gave me some meds to prepare me for the induction the following morning. That was enough to send me into labor, a much-anticipated event. I had contractions all night until around 6:00 am, when he was born.

Max came into the world in his own time and in his own way. We should have known then what a special and unique person he would be.

"We are terrified people will forget him...we're immensely proud of the Run for Max Sam has organized to honor his birthday and life. We're so hopeful we can help to end the epidemic of suicide that's plaguing our young people."

When he was young, his birthday was a lengthy affair. There were friend parties, family parties, special dinners, and numerous gifts. Our friend and neighbor, Mr. John, used to sing, "On the twelfth day of Max's birthday, his parents gave to him..." We wanted to celebrate him, and we included as many family and friends as possible. Obviously, our birthday celebrations looked different as he got older, but we still gathered for at least one special get-together. We wanted our boy to know how much he was cherished and loved.

The hole left in my heart by his death is overwhelming. I know we use that word a lot, but I sometimes feel so overwhelmed I can't breathe. The pain is unfathomable, and I will never be the same. Other parents who have lost children say the same thing.

We are terrified people will forget him. That's why we're immensely proud of the Run for Max Sam has organized to honor Max's birthday and his life. It's a wonderful way to raise money for the American Foundation for Suicide Prevention. We're so hopeful we can help to end the epidemic of suicide that's plaguing our young people.

continued on next page

Max came from my body so it's as if a part of my body has died too.

I was with a friend recently who remarked upon my grief journey. She told me, "Erin, you're working so hard." That statement made me feel both a little proud and a little sad at the same time.

I'm thankful for her encouragement and recognition of all the ways I've tried to deal with Max's death: therapy, support groups, online communities, exercise, time spent with friends, and more. I keep telling people, "I'm just throwing a bunch of shit against the wall to see what sticks." It's an ongoing and sometimes exhausting effort.

Ultimately though, her statement makes me sad—sad that I have to deal with the death of my son at all. What parent wants this? None, of course. It's staggering to deal with all the memories, regrets, anger, and sorrows, and to have to go on with life. At times I haven't wanted to, but I continue to live one day at a time.

Dealing with the loss of a child is something I wouldn't wish on my worst enemy. The pain and heartache are unfathomable. The hole left by Max is immense. I'm finally coming to terms with the fact that I am forever changed by this experience. According to others who have lost a child, I will have pain for the rest of my life. I will think about him every single day until I die. Max came from my body so it's as if a part of my body has died too.

"I'm finally coming to terms with the fact that I am forever changed by this experience."

"...my thoughts, feelings, and responses have changed so dramatically over the past months, it's hard to believe I'm the same person."

I'm believing this more and more. I've felt the hole in my heart, the painful memories in my mind, and the sick feeling in my stomach. His death has impacted me more profoundly than I could have understood or been able to handle at the beginning.

These past sixteen months have been a journey of discovery. I continue to be amazed at how my brain and body have processed my loss. If I had known the day he died, all that I would face and experience in the months to come, I honestly don't think I would have survived. Bit by bit I've experienced new painful revelations about loss, and I suspect I will continue to do so for the rest of my life.

I'm so thankful for the love and support we've gotten since we lost our precious Max. We couldn't have survived without it.

...yesterday clearly revealed the juxtaposition of joy and grief.

Yesterday Sam completed his Run for Max. He got the idea a few months ago, to run twenty-seven miles in honor of what would have been Max's twenty-seventh birthday. He accepted flat donations from people as well as money for every mile he ran over the twenty-seven-mile goal. He ended up running thirty miles and raised more than $21,000 for the American Foundation for Suicide Prevention. We are beyond proud of him for honoring and remembering his brother in such a beautiful way.

It was an emotional day. I was nervous beforehand with concern for Sam, his health, and well being. It's really hard to run twenty-seven plus miles. I was afraid he would push himself until he dropped. I was so touched by the friends and family that came out to support him. One of Sam's friends ran all thirty miles with him while others joined up and dropped out at different points along the route. A group of twenty-five of us met up at a park at the twenty-seventh-mile mark, and had a little celebration honoring Sam and remembering Max.

Sam's girlfriend, Julia, rode on her bike behind the runners all day and carried snacks, drinks, and music to keep them going. Julia's mother, my close friend, made signs with various photos of Max, Sam, and our family. We held those signs along the route as we cheered on Sam and the other runners.

Over the course of the day, I experienced many conflicting emotions. As happy I was for such a successful event, I really just wanted Max to be here. It was an incredibly difficult week. His birthday hit me harder than I anticipated, and then the sadness that overtook me after Sam's run led me to cry myself to sleep.

People keep saying that as time goes on feelings of joy will outweigh feelings of sadness and sorrow. I'm not there yet, but yesterday clearly revealed the juxtaposition of joy and grief. Life is hard. I'm truly thankful for all the people who have joined us in this journey of heartache and grief.

Friendship is love with understanding.

I am sitting here staring at a lovely bouquet of flowers sent to me by friends. This week, I received three bouquets from friends who knew it would be a particularly hard week due to Max's birthday and Sam's Run for Max.

As a gardener, I appreciate the beauty of flowers. They look good, smell good, and make me feel good. Why is it customary to send flowers? How did flowers become a way to express sympathy during a difficult time? We received many flowers and plants following Max's death and still have a few of the house plants.

I'm so thankful for my dear friends who still acknowledge the difficult days I continue to experience since Max's death. Everybody told us that although we were surrounded by people right after Max's death, they would slowly drift away in the months that followed. We've been fortunate to have many strong and solid friends who are still walking alongside us. At the risk of sounding like a broken record, it's been the love and support of these friends and family that have gotten us through the past sixteen months.

There's a proverb that states, "Friendship is love with understanding." There's nothing more powerful than a friend who truly knows me and loves me anyway.

"There's nothing more powerful than a friend who truly knows me and loves me anyway."

I need to get comfortable with figuring out what my new self will look like.

Since Max passed we've been marking the passage of time, month by month. During the first twelve months, we tried to commemorate him in some way, on the third day of each month in remembrance of the day he passed. We haven't done that these last few months. The other day on the third, I didn't even realize the date until the next day. While we no longer consciously recognize the date each month, we still count the months since he left us.

It reminds me of having a baby. We count the baby's age in months, until the age of two, because they change so much during those first twenty-four months. You can't equate a twelve-month-old with a twenty-two-month-old even though they are technically both one-year-olds.

The same is true of grief. Even though I'm only sixteen months into my journey, my thoughts, feelings, and responses have changed so dramatically over the past months, it's hard to believe I'm the same person. Some of the feelings I had in the first few months have dissipated while others have intensified. I can see how that will continue to happen in the months ahead.

I certainly hope that after twenty-four months I will become a bit steadier, but who knows? Again, this is new and unchartered territory. I've finally come to the conclusion that I won't ever get back to my "old self." I need to get comfortable with figuring out what my new self will look like. How will I be different? What will be important? What will be my focus? At this point, I don't know the answers to any of those questions, but I'm at least willing to think about those things. I guess that's progress, right?

A shared experience can so closely bond people together.

Even though we've only been involved with our survivors' group for a few months, the members have become very important to us. We operate like a family rather than a group of strangers with something in common. Isn't it amazing that a shared experience can so closely bond people together?

The other night, one of the members relayed a horrific story of being hospitalized as she was trying to pack up her house and move. As she told her story about the traumatic hospital stay, she lamented all the work she still had ahead of her even though the moving company was coming the following day. She cried because she didn't have anybody to help her, nor did she have the money to pay the movers to do the work for her.

Within minutes, members of our group were offering their help. People immediately sent her money to pay for additional services from the moving company. It was a beautiful and inspiring thing to be part of. The fact that all these people cared enough about her to step in and step up is amazing.

> *"When someone is sharing, you see others nodding their heads in agreement."*

I can't stress enough how helpful it's been for us to be with people, even if only virtually, who truly understand and can relate to what we're feeling. We all know we can say anything to each other and be understood. Over the months, I've shared feelings with friends and family that I know have terrified them or made them feel uncomfortable and helpless. Even though they've wanted to help and comfort me, they can't. Yet our support group is another story. When someone is sharing, you see others nodding their heads in agreement. We understand. We can relate. We're all in this together, and we're here to hold each other up. I'm thankful for this wonderful group of people.

Grief is multifaceted.

I was recently listening to a podcast about grief and loss during menopause. The speakers talked about the grief that can come from changes in your body, lost youth, and the end of childbearing years.

It made me realize that my grief is multifaceted. While my grief over losing Max is the most intense and profound, I also have grief about my parent's failing health. Over the past few years, I've had to grieve their loss little by little. Neither of them is who they once were. Even though they're here physically, they've changed so much that my relationship with them is very different. I'm now more the parent than the child.

I've tried to separate my feelings of grief by saying, "This is related to menopause, while this other thing is related to losing Max, and still a different feeling is related to my parents." As I listened to this podcast, I realized that all my feelings are converging, and I can't really determine which feeling is associated with which situation. Furthermore, attempting to do so is counterproductive. I just need to realize that all these life events are happening simultaneously and have created the "perfect storm." That's what a doctor told me recently.

I'm trying to manage all the feelings of grief I'm experiencing in a variety of ways. Hopefully, something works.

"I can't really determine which feeling is associated with which situation."

Everyone's grief journey is different.

The other night during our support group, a couple who have recently lost their son, shared what it's been like for them since his death. The husband stated, "It's like we're aliens and speak a different language than everyone around us." As usual, his comment was met with a lot of heads nodding in agreement.

We feel the same way. It's as if nobody can understand what we're saying. I think in some cases people are afraid to try and understand because it would mean facing their worst fear. Doesn't every parent secretly fear the loss of a child?

The couple who shared this thought lost their son about three months ago. I admire their willingness to join a survivor's group so soon. Bill and I would not have been able to do so. It's just another example of how everyone's grief journey is different. What works for one person, or couple may not work for another.

continued on next page

Regardless, I've come to value each of the people in the group. I'm so very thankful we are part of it because I know I can say anything, and nobody will judge me or minimize my feelings. I look forward to the day when we can meet some of them in person rather than just virtually.

My faith has been shaken by our loss because I've felt abandoned and betrayed by God.

At the urging of a dear friend, I've rejoined a Bible study this fall. I've been involved in Bible studies for years, but over the past year, I haven't been able to do so. I attribute my lack of desire to lack of concentration and, quite frankly, lack of interest.

The other day, during our group discussion, we had to answer a question about how/when we took a risky stand for God. It was like someone took over my body. I shared about losing Max after eight years of illness despite more prayers than I could count. I shared how we prayed fervently and daily both individually and corporately by organizing numerous prayer meetings with friends and pastors. I went on to tell this group that my faith has been shaken by our loss because I've felt abandoned and betrayed by God. I finished by stating that the risky stand I've taken for God is participating in this Bible study.

After I finished, I looked at the faces of the other women in my group and could read the shock, discomfort, and sympathy on their faces, but only one spoke up. This lovely woman told me how very sorry she was for my loss, and how she wished she could wrap me in her arms to comfort me. Later I received a message from her in which she shared her phone number and told me I could call anytime day or night because she would be honored to serve me in any way she could. She also shared that she was adding me and my family to her daily prayer list.

"We should be Jesus with skin on."

I don't know this woman. I've never laid eyes on her prior to a few weeks ago. The fact that she would respond in such an empathetic and caring way moved me deeply. A concept shared in Christian circles is how we should be "Jesus with skin on." The sentiment is that we can show love and compassion to people around us in the name of Jesus who was the epitome of love and compassion. This dear, faithful woman demonstrated this concept so beautifully to me. I'm thankful she was willing to be "Jesus with skin on" in my life. She helped me to feel a little closer to God during a season when I feel very distant.

Creative activities can be hugely therapeutic.

The book, *It's Okay That You're Not Okay*, by Megan Devine, offers many suggestions on how to help process grief. The author focuses on several creative strategies as a way to face and express our feelings.

She recommends journaling, which I've done, but she suggests an interesting twist. Rather than writing about grief, she suggests writing from the perspective of grief and giving it a voice by asking, "Who are you? Tell me what you feel?" She believes we can learn a lot about ourselves and the pain we're experiencing when we personify our grief.

Another suggestion she makes is to create a collage that reflects how I feel. This exercise could help me to express my grief without words. The author talks about how satisfying it is to tear apart magazines, destroy words and images, and make them into something new and personal.

Yet another creative exercise she offers is "found" poetry. She suggests finding a newspaper or other printed material, like a magazine, book, flyer, or catalog with lots of articles and words,

"Rather than writing about grief, she suggests writing from the perspective of grief and giving it a voice."

getting a highlighter, and scanning the article to underline random words. When finished, she suggests writing down the underlined words or phrases, either leaving them in order or rearranging them into a story that helps to express grief.

I haven't tried any of these exercises yet, but I think I might. I'm intrigued by any activity that will help me express and process my grief. So often I feel so many swirling emotions, it's hard to put a label on them. For me, naming these emotions is the first step in accepting and understanding them. Creative activities, like gardening and cooking, can be hugely therapeutic for me. I'm thankful to be adding a few more activities to my toolbox.[39]

His opinion and perspective challenged me.

Monday was Columbus Day, or as it's also now known, Indigenous Peoples' Day. I remember a day when Max was in 9th or 10th grade, and I asked him if he was excited to be off school on the upcoming Columbus Day. Like many teens, he wasn't enthusiastic about school, so I assumed he was looking forward to a day off.

His response was, "Mom, I'm not going to acknowledge a day that basically celebrates genocide." I was surprised and a little taken aback. I just thought about it as a day to sleep in, but Max was always a little ahead of the curve on things like that.

It was the first time I heard someone negatively talk about Christopher Columbus, highlighting the darker part of his "discovery" of the Americas. When I was in school, history was taught from a Euro-centric viewpoint. I simply learned about the Nina, the Pinta, and the Santa Maria, and the little rhyme, "In 1492, Columbus sailed the ocean blue."

Although Max didn't like being in a school environment, he was an avid learner and was better informed and more well-read at fourteen, than most adults are in their entire lifetime. He had questioned and investigated what he had been taught about our country's history, developed his own view, and wasn't afraid to share it.

I appreciated his opinion and perspective because it challenged me. He took the position that taking into account both the good and bad parts of our nation's history didn't make a person anti-American. Instead, it gave them a more balanced and realistic view of actual events. He was vehemently opposed to hypocrisy of any kind. Let's be honest, there's a lot of it out there.

Max didn't stay on the surface of things. He delved into issues deeply, developed strongly-held and defensible opinions, and cared profoundly about injustices both in current affairs and history. Sometimes his newfound position would contradict my own, and I would get defensive. Over the years I came to understand and appreciate his perspective and I miss it more than I can say.

continued on next page

Emmy is like having a piece of Max.

We now have full custody of Emmy, Max's dog. His girlfriend, Bridget, has begun to have severe allergic reactions to Emmy and informed us a few weeks ago that she would no longer be able to take Emmy for extended periods of time. It was a shock. From our perspective, the shared custody arrangement worked well. Bridget was able to keep Emmy while we traveled, and we were able to spend time with Emmy while we were at home. I love having her with us, and Emmy loves being with us on our property. We have plenty of space to play catch with her, and she's obsessed with her tennis ball. Accepting full-time custody required some quick, out-of-the-box thinking and planning, but we now have a strategy we hope will work for all of us.

Honestly, I'm glad we will have Emmy with us more often. She's a great dog: smart, obedient, eager to please, and loving. Plus, she's a huge comfort to me. Emmy is like having a piece of Max with us and giving her up would be like losing him all over again.

Ultimately, I'm thankful for full-time custody and for friends who intervened to help come up with a workable plan. Emmy has been a true blessing to me, and I'm very grateful to have her.

"I don't want anyone living with mental illness or their family members to feel alone."

Let's talk about mental health as openly and freely as we talk about physical health.

This past weekend I visited my college alma mater for the first time in many years. I was able to see dear friends and reconnect with many I haven't seen since I left. I had great conversations with beautiful, strong, courageous women who have been through difficult times. It was so refreshing that most people I encountered were authentic. Perhaps at our age, we've finally learned there's no reason to put on a mask. It's too exhausting to pretend like life is perfect.

My biggest takeaway is that our children are struggling and suffering. I heard story after story of teens and young adults suffering with depression, anxiety, anorexia, suicide ideation, and more. It seems the incidences of mental illness are skyrocketing, particularly in young people. I don't know if it's due to the pandemic, all the fearmongering that's so prevalent in our society, social media, the twenty-four-hour news cycle, or other factors, but we can't ignore it any longer.

Since Max passed, I've tried to become an advocate of sorts for mental illness awareness. We struggled for years with Max's health issues, and we were mostly transparent about them. Yet I fully understand why so many people are suffering in silence. I think many fear judgment and marginalization of their condition or that of a loved one. Maybe, too, they don't know where to turn.

I guess that's one way I can honor Max. I can keep talking about mental illness to help reduce the stigma. I can direct people to crisis text lines and hotlines where they can get help.

I don't want anyone living with mental illness or their family members to feel alone. Recently, I heard a woman talking about her partner whom she lost to suicide. She said he was very open about his struggles, and they had many conversations about his mental illness. During one of these conversations, he told her, "If I had stage-four cancer, you wouldn't hold my death against me. Well, it's like I have stage-four mental illness. If I die from it, why would you hold my death against me?" When put in those terms, it makes a lot of sense.

Let's all be more transparent and talk about mental health as openly and freely as we talk about physical health. Let's help people to find therapists, psychiatrists, support groups, and other programs to assist them in dealing with their mental illness. Let's work together to bring an end to the stigma and to help those who are struggling.

Everyone who has lost a child fears the same thing–that our child will be forgotten.

One of the most difficult things to navigate since Max passed has been the friends and family who don't want to talk about him. People close to us have ignored difficult days like his birthday, Christmas, and Mother's and Father's Day. We've heard excuses like:

"I didn't want to upset you by bringing it up."

"I can't talk about him. I can't even think about him."

"I didn't know what to say."

"I didn't even realize today/yesterday was ________."

I call these statements excuses because that's exactly what they are. People who love us and loved him should be the very people who talk about him. After all, they knew him best.

"We will never forget him, so we don't want anyone else to forget him either."

Everyone who has lost a child fears the same thing—that our child will be forgotten. It's like adding insult to injury. We will never forget him, so we don't want anyone else to forget him either. I have a feeling that will be my role for the rest of my life, to talk about Max and keep his memory alive.

I have a friend who lost a son ten years ago. Since then, his siblings have gone on to have a whole gaggle of children. Each of these children talks about their uncle as if they knew him. They tell stories about him as if it is their own memory they're sharing. I find this so inspiring and beautiful.

When Sam has children, I will make it my goal to tell them so much about Max that they will feel like they knew him too. It's the least I can do to keep his memory alive.

Max loved Emmy deeply. I know he found her as comforting, loving, and intuitive as I do.

Emmy and I have been working with a dog trainer. This young woman knows her stuff. We've been working on obedience, short commands, and walking. One of the primary techniques has been to teach Emmy "place." This is where she should go and remain when I say the word "place" particularly when someone comes to the door and/or she becomes very excited. We moved Emmy's dog bed downstairs for this purpose, so we can train her using a physical object as her "place."

continued on next page

Since I'm too lazy to drag her bed upstairs every night, I considered getting her another dog bed for our bedroom. Instead, I chose an old comforter from the linen closet for her to sleep on. It was an old, black comforter that belonged to Max. I folded it up and placed it on the floor in our bedroom. The very first night Emmy went directly to the comforter, sniffed it a bit, and then lay down on it.

I guess it might have just looked like a dog bed to her, but I'm choosing to believe that she could still smell Max's scent. According to some estimates, a dog's sense of smell is more than 10,000 times better than ours, so I don't think it's out of the question that she could still smell her dad, our sweet Max. Max loved Emmy deeply. I know he found her as comforting, loving, and intuitive as I do. She was good for him, and he was good for her. I feel close to him when I see her laying on his old comforter.

We fool ourselves into believing nothing bad will happen to us.

When I was pregnant with Max, I read the book, *What to Expect When You're Expecting.*[40] I was trying to prepare myself for what would happen during my pregnancy and delivery. As comprehensive as the book was, there were still things I experienced that made me shout, "Why didn't anybody tell me about this?" About the fact that nothing can be done to precipitate labor when a baby is two weeks late, or about the pain associated with episiotomy stitches, or how much breastfeeding would hurt at first.

I've decided we need a book titled *What to Expect When You're Grieving*. Nobody talks about grief, or if they do, we usually tune them out. In our self-sufficient, power-of-positive-thinking culture, we fool ourselves into believing nothing bad will happen to us if we follow the formula for a safe and happy life. When

"In our 'I can fix anything' world, many view grief as something to get through, something to get over.

In reality, grief is something to be experienced, hopefully, with the love and support of others."

For these reasons, I'm writing this book. I want to save people the confusion, discouragement, surprise, and sadness I've felt over regular, normal aspects of grieving.

I want them to know that grieving is not just emotional, it's mental and physical too. I want to tell them that grief is unique and personal. Everybody does not grieve in the same way, nor is every loss equal. Loss of a grandparent is not equal to the loss of a child. Divorce is not the same as the death of a spouse. Let's stop trying to equalize things that aren't equal.

I want people to know that grief is not a problem to be solved. In our "I can fix anything" world, many view grief as something to get through, something to get over. If you don't do it quick enough or well enough, there must be something wrong with you. In reality, grief is something to be experienced, hopefully, with the love and support of others.

The bottom line is we view our emotional and mental pain as either an anomaly or an opportunity. We either think it's a deviation from normal so we try to get back to "normal" as quickly as possible, or we think it's an opportunity to learn something and become a "better" person because of it. In reality, pain is just a fact of life. Every last one of us will experience pain at some point in our lives. If we begin to talk about death, loss, and grief as commonly as we do other facts of life, perhaps we can normalize something that's already normal, to begin with. We just don't like to admit it.

Control is an illusion, and there is no formula for a safe, happy, and healthy life.

Recently, I've heard people use the phrase, "He/she is living his/her best life." It means to me that the person has mastered life and is thriving. Every time I hear someone use this phrase I want to scream.

I don't know if it's just jealousy because I'm clearly NOT living my best life now. How could I when I've lost my son? Or perhaps it bothers me because it implies a level of control over our lives that simply doesn't exist. I mean seriously, who has mastered life? We'd all like to think that security, happiness, and health can be ours if only we make the right choices and do the right things, but that's simply not true.

Max's death has taught me that control is an illusion, and there is no formula for a safe, happy, and healthy life. Can we just stop pretending? We can do all the "right" things and make all the "right" decisions and still random, catastrophic, life-changing things can happen to us.

"We believe if we had been more diligent, involved, or capable we could have prevented our loved one from dying."

We pretend that good things happen when we're good, and we secretly believe that bad things happen because we're bad and must have done something wrong. I think this is why so many of us struggle when we experience a catastrophic loss. We honestly think we must be to blame, that we are somehow guilty. Guilt is common, particularly among those of us who have lost a loved one to suicide, but guilt is really about control. We believe if we had been more diligent, involved, or capable we could have prevented our loved one from dying. I am beginning to think we're all control freaks, every last one of us.

"The LORD is close to the brokenhearted."

PSALMS 34:18

The screen saver on my laptop is a picture of Bill and me from our vow renewal in August 2017. In the picture, we're holding hands with huge smiles on our faces as we prepare to walk down the aisle for the ceremony. Max gave a toast after the ceremony and Sam said the prayer before dinner. We were surrounded by beloved family and friends. It was one of the most special days in memory.

The following day, I was overcome with gratitude at the multitude of our blessings. We had an incredibly special weekend. We had two beautiful boys who honored us with their words, dear friends came from near and far to celebrate with us, and beloved

family who shared in the special day. I was so overwhelmed with love and thanksgiving that my eyes welled up with tears.

It's been a long time since I've felt that kind of gratitude. We still have many of the same blessings as we did that special weekend, but Max's death overshadows them all. Is this selfish, ungrateful, sinful? Maybe it's a bit of all three but that's how I feel.

Last night I attended a women's ministry event at a local church. It was a night of worship, prayer, teaching, and testimony. One of the worship leaders shared her testimony about losing her brother to suicide as a young adult. She talked about her feelings of anger towards God and told us at one point she literally shrieked over God's failure to save her brother. I could relate to every word she said. She also told us in retrospect, she could see

"It's been a very long time since I've felt that kind of gratitude."

the Lord walking beside her throughout her ordeal. At the time, however, she felt abandoned, betrayed, and alone. We could feel the same, regardless of what we were experiencing.

It made me think about a bible verse I prayed regularly while Max was sick, Psalms 34:18, "The LORD is close to the brokenhearted; He rescues those whose spirits are crushed." I haven't thought about or prayed that verse since Max passed, but it's more applicable now than ever. Perhaps if I pray it, I may begin to feel the Lord's presence and His restoration of my spirit.

Feelings are funny. On one hand, I keep hearing it's important to fully experience my feelings, that it's part of the healing process. On the other hand, I've been hearing for years that feelings are fickle and not to be trusted. Instead, I should trust in the promises of God. Which is it? Are feelings valid or deceiving? I think the answer may be both.

At the end of the event, a friend with whom I was sitting, slipped me a note she had written during our prayer time. She wrote, "You may not think it, but you are a testimony that Jesus has been by your side… the pain, the loss, the hours of sadness you've been through... it can only be Jesus." I later told her, I don't "think" it, and I certainly don't "feel" it, but I'm trying. We've all heard the phrase, "Fake it 'til you make it." Maybe eventually I'll get to the point where I can clearly feel Jesus' presence, feel gratitude, and feel joy. I'm not there now, but maybe one day I'll "make it."

Let's instead focus on a cycle of grief, rather than stages.

Once and for all, let's throw out the concept of "stages of grief." The widely accepted five stages of grief: denial, anger, bargaining, depression, and acceptance, were developed by Elisabeth Kubler-Ross in the late 60s, after years of working with terminally ill patients. In this population, the stages make sense as a way for a person to deal with their own impending death.

However, these stages should never have been applied universally to grief. Other types of loss are very different from one's own impending death. When dealing with the loss of a child, the stages of bargaining and acceptance are most unrealistic. Bargaining makes sense when a person wants to change an impending outcome but is much less reasonable when dealing with a loss that's already occurred. What can bargaining possibly accomplish in this scenario? Nothing. It's counterproductive and hurtful.

"It's ludicrous to me to think a person should move step by step through stages of grief, never to revisit a prior one."

The other stage that's almost cruel to suggest is acceptance. I've asked myself, "What does acceptance of a child's death even look like?" The word acceptance has connotations of agreement and approval. I will never agree with Max's death, much less approve of it.

And can we talk about the term "stages?" Stages indicate a movement through something, a step in a process. It infers that a person moves from one stage to the next never to return to the previous one. For example, in the stages of child development where children move from infant to toddler to preschooler and so on, it would be ludicrous to believe a child could go back and redo a previous stage, right?

It is just as ludicrous to me to think a person should move like a robot, step by step through stages of grief, never to revisit a prior one. I'm not a robot and my feelings have been anything but linear. By holding up the Kubler-Ross Five Stages of Grief as the gold standard, we are setting up people who have lost a loved one, for confusion, discouragement, despair, hopelessness, and more. Let's instead focus on a *cycle* of grief, rather than *stages*, where a person can revisit an emotion time and time again over the course of their lifetime. Because a lifetime is how long our grief will last.

Many of us secretly think of God as a cosmic genie.

Today in church our pastor talked about "the dark night of the soul," a period of utter spiritual desolation, disconnection, and emptiness in which one feels totally separated from God. The phrase was coined in the 16th century by poet and Catholic mystic, St. John of the Cross in the poem, "Las Noche Oscura del Alma (The Dark Night of the Soul)."

Apparently, the dark night of the soul usually occurs later in a person's spiritual journey and usually follows a tragic event that makes us question our previously held beliefs. This spiritual depression can lead to questions like, "What is the meaning of life? Why do good people suffer? Is there even a God?"

I am in the midst of a dark night of my soul. Since Max died, I've felt abandoned and betrayed by God, and my faith has been seriously shaken. I've wondered how to reconcile a good God with such a horrific event, the loss of my beloved child. I've also questioned whether I can trust God again.

While Max was struggling, I fervently prayed for his healing and deliverance. My faith was steadfast and strong. Since his death, it's been a different story. Apparently, many of us secretly think of God as a cosmic genie who must grant our wish if we pray correctly. I used to scoff at this idea, and I honestly thought my faith was superior and far stronger. I believed my faith was rooted in solid, orthodox theology. I guess I was wrong.

Our pastor mentioned that many people come through the dark night of the soul with a stronger faith because it often leads to a spiritual awakening. I hope that's true for me, but at this point, I can't say for certain it will happen. I'm still too discouraged and angry. I'm attending church and Bible study but without much passion or enthusiasm. I'm hoping that as time goes on, I will again feel close to God. I KNOW He hasn't forgotten about or abandoned me. I just hope that eventually, my feelings catch up.

A Celebration of Life in Photos

August-October

"The LORD is close to the brokenhearted; He rescues those whose spirits are crushed."

-Psalms 34:18

Max at Kids Zone, 2001

Max's Christmas gift to me, 2012

Max's Sketch for Bill

Max @ 15 Months

the Run for Max

at the finish line

NOVEMBER

There's nothing like a devastating loss to reveal the fragility of life.

I just finished Kate Bowler's new book, *No Cure for Being Human.*[41] Kate is a professor of religion at Duke's Divinity School and was diagnosed with stage four colon cancer in 2015. She has lived with a terminal illness ever since.

Kate has a unique perspective about living in a world uncomfortable with existing pain. People in our culture attempt to avoid pain at all costs and/or get through it as quickly as possible. We tend to be okay with a person who is on the other side of pain, but much less comfortable with a person who is in the middle of it.

> *"We tend to be okay with a person who is on the other side of pain, but much less comfortable with a person who is in the middle of it."*

Kate's cancer could return at any moment. She doesn't have any guarantees she will see her son graduate from high school, attend his wedding, or grow old with her husband. As a matter of fact, it's very likely she won't get to do any of those things due to the nature of her illness.

None of us have guarantees in life, but we, as Americans, like to think we do. We like to imagine that life will go along according to our plan. But for those of us who have had the rug pulled out from under us, life is a different story. We know that tragedy can befall us at any time because it already has. There's nothing like a devastating loss to reveal the fragility of life. Kate says it best, "We all live like this, without assurance, without formulas, desperate for the secret to carry on."

Over the last year and a half, I've written a lot about hope. As a matter of fact, many of these reflections mention hope. So often, since Max died, I've thought, "Will I ever hope again? If so, when will it return?" Apparently, Kate feels the same way. She writes in her book, "What if I can't learn to hope again?" Deep down, I share the same fear.

My grief colors everything I see.

Last night I led the discussion at book club on the book I had recommended, *The Last Thing He Told Me*, by Laura Dave.[42] The story is about a father who mysteriously disappears and leaves his 16-year-old daughter in the care of his new wife, a stepmom with whom she wants nothing to do. It was a riveting storyline with many twists and turns. I enjoyed it a great deal and was anxious to discuss it with everybody.

The discussion seemed to revolve around whether it was fair and right for the father to leave his daughter's safety and well-being in the hands of another. The consensus was that it wasn't fair of

continued on next page

him to put his new wife in this predicament, nor was it right to leave his daughter behind. Most in the group agreed that a parent should never leave a child, no matter the reason.

Our discussion made me think once again about the illusion of control we have as parents. Deep down we believe we should be able to manage everything that happens to our children so we can keep them safe. I think the default position for most parents is to feel responsible for and in control of what happens to our kids. We honestly think it's up to us to ensure their health and well-being, not only in childhood but beyond. Believe me, I get it. I once felt the same.

I've learned the hard way that I couldn't ensure Max's health and well-being. I learned that I couldn't protect him or keep him safe. As much as I wanted to save him, I couldn't. This is the reality I live with every day now.

Last night I felt like our group was a little too hard on this fictional father. I felt like he was in an impossible situation, and he made the only choice he thought he could. Mine was definitely the minority view.

I now often find my outlook to be in the minority. My grief colors everything I see, so it stands to reason that I would see things differently from other parents who haven't lost a child. I wonder if my grief will always alter my view, or if I will eventually be able to see things through a different lens. Only time will tell.

"I wonder if my grief will always alter my view."

We love them fiercely from the moment they're born and just as passionately throughout their lives.

When Max was a baby, we often read the book, *Love You Forever*, by Robert Munsch.[43] Both my mom and I would read it to him while he snuggled in our lap. There's a line that's repeated throughout the book that reads, "I'll love you forever, I'll like you for always. As long as I'm living my baby you'll be." Rather than just read this line, I used to sing it. However, I could never get through it without my voice cracking. Every time Max heard the emotion in my voice he would tilt his head back and look up at me. I can still see his sweet, chubby face with curiosity and concern reflected in his eyes.

Doesn't this line so accurately describe how we feel about our children? We love them fiercely from the moment they're born and just as passionately throughout their lives. They may grow up but deep down we always think of them as our babies.

Up to the end of his life, I called Max "Lovey," "My love," and "Baby." I would often tell him, "You'll always be my baby." Usually, he rolled his eyes at this sentiment, but I think he secretly liked it. Don't we all like hearing how much we are loved and cherished?

Even though he's been gone for almost a year and a half, I still love and cherish him. I always will. Memories like the one of him sitting in my lap reading a book, while I kissed and smelled his beautiful head, bring tears to my eyes. They're priceless. I hope Max knows that I'll love him forever, I'll like him for always and as long as I'm living, he will be my baby.

I know how tempting it is to use anything to numb the pain, but I also know that doesn't work for long.

On a recent trip, I sat next to a man on a plane who began chatting with me the moment I sat down. I usually prefer to read while traveling rather than chat with my neighbors, but he really didn't give me a choice. He told me all about his family, his home, and his plans to attend a golf tournament for the weekend. As we talked, he pulled out his phone to show me pictures of his wife and kids. His youngest was a chubby baby boy.

As I admired the pictures, I inquired about the ages of all his children. He informed me that they had lost their baby boy seven months earlier due to SIDS. I was shocked and heartbroken for him. I expressed my sympathy and told him about losing Max. In the next breath, he shared that he'd also lost a twenty-year-old daughter in July 2020. We both sat there stunned at our shared, horrific losses.

I asked how he and his wife were doing, if they were in counseling or a support group, and if they'd read any helpful books on grief. He told me his wife was taking the loss of their baby boy particularly hard, but that he was doing okay. He mentioned that he didn't "go for therapy and support groups" because he used "joints and Jameson" to cope. I laughed and said, "Well, whatever works" but my heart was broken for him.

Believe me, I know how tempting it is to use something, anything to numb the pain, but I also know that doesn't work for long. Eventually, the pain surfaces and is oftentimes worse than before. Feelings that get suppressed, get expressed, usually in unhealthy and unproductive ways.

"Eventually, the pain surfaces..."

I don't know what will happen with this man and his wife. If neither is dealing with their feelings, I don't have much hope for their marriage. Marriage is hard enough without adding a devastating wedge like the loss of a child. I pray they seek help. I pray they won't continue to numb their feelings. I hope they stay together for the sake of their other children.

Bill and I have taken productive steps to deal with our grief, and still, things are hard. Our grief if like a living, breathing thing between us, and given the chance it can drive us apart. We're trying not to let that happen. I guess my hopes and prayers for this other couple apply to us as well. I hope we make it. I think we will.

Today at church, I felt Him gently pulling me closer.

I've been ignoring Jesus since Max died. I recently told my therapist that I believe He is patiently waiting for me to decide whether I can trust Him again. I really believe He's okay with my doubt, anger, and distance, and wants me to know He'll be waiting when I'm ready to re-engage.

Today at church, I felt Him gently pulling me closer. Each worship song we sang spoke to His character, a reminder I desperately needed. One song assured me that He fights on my behalf. Another song confirmed that nothing is too big or difficult for Him to handle, He can literally move mountains. A third song reminded me that He is with me in my heartache and weeping. That final song brought me to tears.

I could count on one hand the number of times I've felt Jesus' presence over the last eighteen months. It's not because He hasn't been there but because I haven't been paying attention.

continued on next page

I've ensconced myself in grief like a coat of armor, not allowing anything to penetrate it.

Today was a beautiful reminder that Jesus does indeed want me to return to His loving, comforting arms. I'm just so thankful He's not as fickle as I am. I'm grateful He continues to pursue me, despite my anger and apathy. I think I can envision my returning to a vibrant relationship with Him. I believe I'll eventually get back to Him and when I do, He'll joyfully embrace me. Thank you for your patience and love, Jesus.

By focusing on his restoration and our ultimate reunion in Heaven, I think I will be able to come through the darkness of my grief.

Yesterday I met a gentleman who has recently lost two loved ones. He told me about his beliefs in karma, reincarnation, psychic mediums, and positive energy, and how they have helped him in dealing with his losses. He asked me if I'd consulted a medium to speak with Max, believed in reincarnation, and/or practiced sending positive energy to Max to help him "cross over to the other side." I answered no to all his questions.

I'm not criticizing his beliefs; I just don't happen to share them. However, I understand the attraction of *anything* that may help us feel connected to our loved one and comforted about their loss.

"I understand the attraction of anything that may help us feel connected to our loved one and comforted about their loss."

His suggestion about positive energy has me thinking though. Since Max died, I have had a difficult time talking to him. When I do, I usually weep and say, "Why did you leave me? I miss you!" This gentleman told me that personally he's happy his loved ones are no longer suffering. He said that when he sees them in his dreams they are young, healthy, and vibrant. That picture resonated with me. Max was young and vibrant, but he certainly wasn't healthy. His depression and epilepsy had taken a toll on his body and mind, so the thought of him fully restored in Heaven is comforting. This gentleman also claimed that when we're despondent and crying all the time, we are hurting the one we lost. They don't want us to be depressed, they want us to be happy. He suggested that our sorrow is about us, not them.

This morning when I woke up, I told Max, "I'm glad you aren't suffering anymore, my love. I'm glad you're at peace. I miss you but I'm one day closer to seeing your beautiful face again." I'm going to try and expend more positive energy when I think about and talk to Max, not because I believe it will help Max but because it will help me. By focusing on his restoration and our ultimate reunion in Heaven, I think I will be able to come through the darkness of my grief.

Trauma is the reason for our unhealthy coping mechanisms. It keeps us stuck.

When Max was about seven months old, he appeared in a Father's Day advertisement for a local retailer for whom I worked. The company's marketing director knew I had recently had a baby and asked me if I'd allow him to be photographed for the ad. It was Max's modeling debut.

My mom and I took Max to the photoshoot, and we were bursting with pride. Finally, everyone would see just how beautiful our sweet Max was.

The photoshoot included a young couple, the mom and dad, and Max. The photographer wanted the man to hold Max since the advertisement was for Father's Day. Every time this man held Max in his arms, Max began to wail. We tried everything to soothe him and get him to smile but to no avail. The photo that was ultimately selected for the ad was of Max being held against the "Father's" chest with his face turned toward the side. From that angle, it was hard to tell he was crying.

We decided after this exhausting and less than successful photoshoot that Max's modeling career started and ended that day. While I wanted the world to see my beautiful baby, I didn't want to subject him to the trauma of another photoshoot with strangers. In retrospect, he experienced far greater trauma throughout his life than just a photoshoot gone awry. He experienced bullying in school, seizures, and debilitating depression. We experienced trauma due to the many crises and ultimately his death.

Trauma is a hot topic lately because we all experience it at some point in our lives, and it impacts us in serious ways. Oftentimes, trauma is the reason for our unhealthy coping mechanisms. It keeps us stuck.

Trauma is a big topic of conversation in our survivors' support group. Everyone acknowledges that suicide isn't just about loss, it's also about trauma. One woman told me recently that she's heard the trauma related to suicide is second only to that experienced by concentration camp survivors. I don't know if that's accurate, but it certainly speaks to the horror of suicide for those of us left behind.

> *"Everyone acknowledges that suicide isn't just about loss, it's also about trauma."*

I'm really trying to face and deal with my trauma, but it's complex, multilayered, and multifaceted. I'm hopeful that with the help of my therapists, I'll deal with it. I'm also glad that my sweet Max doesn't have to deal with his trauma any longer.

Our grief will not diminish over time. Our capacity for other things will simply increase.

Recently while in Florida, we held a gathering of local people from our support group. Sam was in town, and he wanted to meet some of the people he's been getting to know via Zoom for the last several months.

Even though we were meeting some of these people for the first time in person, there already existed a level of commonality and comfort with them. Our shared experience has bonded us in a deep way. As everyone was talking and laughing in small groups, one of the members said, "Look at all of us. We seem so normal but we're not." I knew exactly what he meant. None of us are "normal" anymore. We'll never be normal again.

continued on next page

"None of us are "normal" anymore. We'll never be normal again."

Grief has changed us permanently. None of us will ever be the same and I think this is difficult for others to understand. Everybody else wants us to go back to being the way we were before our traumatic and catastrophic loss, but that's simply not possible.

Through our support group, I've learned some of the following lessons about grief and it's helped me to feel less alone:

- Our grief is as unique as our fingerprint.
- Although we may not get to the point of *acceptance* of our loved one's death, we can get to the point of *acknowledgment*.
- Our guilt can be reframed as regret. It's not our fault that our loved one is gone.
- The only thing we're guilty of is loving too much.
- Expecting others to understand our grief is like expecting to get oranges from an apple tree.
- Our grief will not diminish over time. Our capacity for other things will simply increase.
- It's like we're aliens and now speak a different language than everybody around us.
- Every day is one day closer to seeing our loved one.
- We can eliminate "coulda,' oughta,' woulda' and shoulda'" (COWS) from our vocabulary.
- Losing a child is like losing a limb, a part of you is missing forever.
- Every one of us fears that our loved one will be forgotten.
- People will tell you that you're strong even though you feel incredibly weak.

These lessons have been invaluable and I'm so thankful for all the brave men and women who have gone before us. They have shown us that life can go on, that joy is possible again. Some of these people have been part of the support group for more than ten years, and their love and encouragement for us newbies is incredible. Without this kind of wisdom, support and camaraderie, I doubt we could go on.

Perhaps the blanket of grief that's been covering me since Max died is slowly receding.

This morning I was sitting on my lanai in Florida. Bill and I decided to spend Thanksgiving here again, and we've been here for several weeks. As I was enjoying my morning coffee and reading, I began to notice a bird squawking nearby. As I looked up and around, I saw a black bird perched on the power lines behind our house. He kept repeating, "Squawk" and then a pause, and then "Squawk" followed by another pause. He did this for a couple of minutes and it seemed to me that he was saying, "Mom," and then a pause, and then "Mom," followed by another pause. It may sound crazy but I'm choosing to believe it was my Max.

After he got my attention, I started to talk to him. I said, "Good morning, my love. I see you. I hear you. I miss you." I went on to say a few more things to him. Instead of squawking just once and pausing, he started to chirp, "Squawk, Squawk, Squawk, Squawk." It seemed as if he were saying, "I love you, Mom." It brought tears to my eyes, and I repeated back, "I love you too, Maxie."

"It seemed as if he were saying, 'I love you, Mom.'"

Even as I write this, I realize how strange it sounds, but I'm choosing to believe that this bird was a visit from my precious son. It has been many months since I've seen the bird that first appeared after Max passed. Although the bird this morning was different, I'm choosing to believe it was still a sign from my beloved boy to let me know that he's okay and he's watching over me. Words can not express the comfort this brings me.

There's no shortage of birds in Florida. There are birds everywhere. Flocks of them fly overhead and roost in nearby trees making a racket, but this bird was different somehow. First of all, it was alone. Second, I honestly felt as if it was repeatedly trying to get my attention. I'm so thankful I was aware enough to notice him and have a brief but meaningful conversation.

Hopefully, I'm in a place where I can notice things like this more often. Perhaps the blanket of grief that's been covering me since Max died is slowly receding. It's not gone, but maybe it's not covering my entire body anymore. Maybe I'll be more aware of what's going on around me rather than just stuck in my own head and my own grief.

One of the things I've been working on over the last several months is mindfulness. Mindfulness is simply being aware of and appreciating what's happening now. It's about living in and focusing on the present rather than living in the past or the future. It sounds so simple, yet I find it so challenging to practice. And practice is what it takes. If you're anything like me, you spend a lot of time thinking about the past either romanticizing it or regretting it. Or you may be more focused on the future, either worrying about what will happen or looking forward to an event or an easier season of life. To truly be present in the moment and use your five senses to appreciate and simply notice what's happening right now is hard. Hopefully, I'll get better at practicing mindfulness. That's my wish for you too. We'd all be better off if we did.

"Mindfulness is simply being aware of and appreciating what's happening now."

November

Hudson Blechmnas + Pittsburgh Blechmans, 2019

Wedding of Family Friends

University of Akron Soccer Game, 2019

Max, 2019

Mindfulness is about living in and focusing on the present rather than living in the past or the future.

A FEW TIPS THAT HAVE HELPED ME *along the way*

My journey in the last eighteen months since Max died has been the hardest of my life. Perhaps that's an understatement, but when Max first passed, I honestly had no idea about all the emotions and struggles I would face over the coming months. Looking back, I had some unrealistic expectations and plain old ignorance about the grief process. Maybe this is a good thing. If I had known the magnitude of all I would have to deal with, I probably would have been overwhelmed to the point of paralysis. **If you find yourself on a similar journey or walking alongside someone who has experienced a devastating loss, I'd like to offer some tips that have helped me along the way.**

THERAPISTS

Individual counseling is invaluable. Find a counselor with whom you click and see them as often as necessary. I saw mine weekly for the first several months, then bi-weekly after that. I anticipate needing ongoing support and don't plan on stopping anytime soon. Stick with counseling as long as necessary.

SUPPORT GROUPS

It took us a year to join a support group, but I'm certain we would have benefited greatly from starting sooner. Being with a group of people who have experienced and understand the same loss, is validating, normalizing, and comforting. It will help you feel less alone. There are in-person groups, virtual groups, and even online forums to connect with others who've experienced a loss like you. I'd encourage you to check them out and join one.

MARRIAGE COUNSELING

If you have a spouse or partner, find a good marriage counselor. The strain a devastating loss puts on a relationship cannot be overstated. I'm certain Bill and I wouldn't have made it through the last eighteen months without the counsel, support, and guidance of our marriage therapist.

CREATIVE OUTLETS

I've found gardening, cooking, and journaling to be immensely helpful in dealing with and processing my emotions. If you have a creative outlet you already enjoy, try engaging in it more frequently. It's therapeutic. If you don't have one, try to find something like painting, knitting, sculpting, crafting, or home improvement projects to name just a few.

MEDICATION

Don't be afraid to consider medication to help you deal with your loss. Many of us have had to seek medical intervention to help us manage our daily lives. Taking medication is not a sign of weakness but rather a sign of strength and wisdom. Speak to your doctor about a medication that can help you cope, sleep, and function in the face of your tragic loss.

DON'T NUMB YOUR FEELINGS

The ways in which we can numb our feelings are vast: busyness, TV/movies, exercise, work, shopping, alcohol/drugs, and more. When faced with severe pain, it's tempting to try to avoid, numb, or ignore it. This doesn't work, believe me. The only way through your loss is to face and deal with all the emotions you will experience.

REFRAME EXPECTATIONS

A sudden, devastating loss sends us reeling. Like me, you may have limited experience with loss and may set unrealistic expectations for yourself. Be patient and compassionate with yourself and your grief journey. It is long and painful, and you may have to readjust your expectations along the way. It's okay. Your grief journey will likely be different from others. Be gentle with yourself and don't fall into the trap of following someone else's timetable.

BE HONEST

Share how you're feeling with your family and close friends. Nobody can read your mind and the people who really love you want to know how to best help. Your honesty will allow them to do that. Be honest with yourself. Your feelings will come out one way or another, so you may as well face and mourn your loss.

When I first thought about compiling all these reflections into a book, I believed I would be able to wrap it up with a nice, neat bow. I'm not sure if that was wishful or delusional thinking, but it's just not possible. There's nothing nice or neat about facing such a devastating loss. As is the case for me, surviving your loss may very well be the hardest thing you will ever deal with. I suppose the best we can hope for is that with God's help and the support of others we will make it. That's my prayer for both of us.

FINAL THOUGHTS *for your journey*

I don't know about you, but I appreciate honesty, authenticity, and vulnerability. There's enough posturing and pretending going on in the world and, dare I say, in Christian circles. Even though we know other people's lives aren't perfect, we often can't see beyond the picture-perfect social media posts or carefully cultivated masks people wear. I personally find it exhausting.

That's one of the reasons I've written this book. I want others to know how messy, unpredictable, and soul-crushing a loss can be. I want to cut through the platitudes and over-spiritualization that is so common in Christian circles. I want people to know faith, fear, and doubt can exist in the same mind and heart. I want people to know there's no timetable for grieving, and expectations can be paralyzing.

I just skimmed an article about how the trend of public confession and self-deprecation is keeping us more focused on our brokenness than on our redemption and restoration as believers. I vehemently disagree.

I became a Christian in the nineties, and I raised my boys with what I hoped would bring health, happiness, and holiness. Family devotions, mission statements, purity pledges, and other recommended practices were present in our home. None of those are an issue in and of themselves, but when we expect them to fit into a formula that guarantees specific results, we're setting ourselves up for heartache. There is no formula or particular parenting method that guarantees your children will always be okay. Friends, as hard as it is to accept this, we must. It will allow us to be more open with our desires and insecurities. It will provide a way for us to ask for and receive real support. Jesus did not shy away from speaking the truth, and we need to do a better job of being authentic ourselves.

"...when we expect them to fit into a formula that guarantees specific results, we're setting ourselves up for heartache."

"Jesus did not shy away from speaking the truth, and we need to do a better job of being authentic ourselves."

If you're still reading this book you likely share my appreciation for authenticity. Maybe you too are tired of pretending and crave a community where you can just be real. Yes, we have victory and redemption in Christ, AND we live in a broken and hurting world. So, it stands to reason that we would be broken and hurting as well. We CAN expect full restoration when we get to Heaven, but until then we may find ourselves dealing with unexpected and devastating loss. We can survive that loss and live with joy again, but it's a messy and painful journey. What's helped me the most are the communities and relationships in which I've been able to be real about my pain, about my suffering, about my shattered illusions of control,

"I walk around with a huge hole in my heart and yet I'm learning how to still appreciate and enjoy the life I've been given."

about my grief. I'm all for public confession and self-deprecation because I believe in the power of authenticity.

None of us like living in tension, but that's exactly what living without the person we've lost is like. I miss Max every day. I walk around with a huge hole in my heart and yet I'm learning how to still appreciate and enjoy the life I've been given. I don't know if it's possible for anyone to master this tension, but I pray we all do. I have no doubt it will be the hardest thing we've ever done but with the grace and love of Jesus, I believe it's possible.

There's a phrase I keep seeing on jewelry, coffee mugs, T-shirts, and the like that says, "Beautiful girl, you can do hard things." I think this applies to all of us. Let me leave you with this phrase, "(Insert your name), you can do hard things." With Jesus' help, we can do it! May God bless you!

You can do hard things.

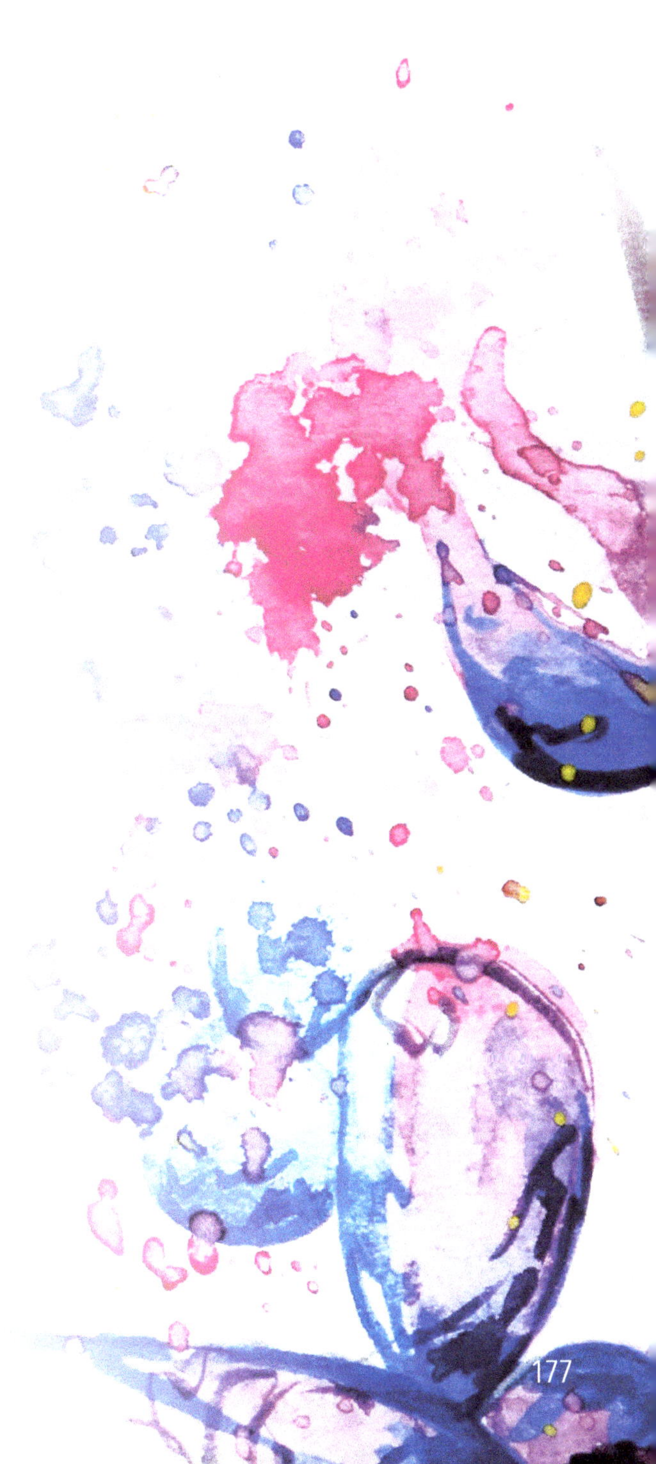

four years later

Bill's perspective

(Max's dad)

FOUR YEARS LATER

MY DREADED JOURNEY

Time is an amazing thing.

It gives you new perspectives. It softens the edges of pain slowly but surely. It blurs past events in a way that makes life's tragedies more tolerable. Because certainly, for us, the loss of Max was intolerable. Somehow my brain—my spirit—created a bubble around itself for the first few moments and days after his death. I believe this is how God and human evolution work to help us survive such impossible shock and sudden loss. But then time passes, and in some ways four years seems like a century.

Why am I calling it my "dreaded journey?" For me, the tragedy of losing Max wasn't sudden. The realization this outcome was possible had started years before. The moment I realized Max was in serious trouble was two weeks into his freshman year in college. He called us around 2 a.m. with the police in his dorm room. He was having his first episode of suicide ideation and was wise enough to call 911. We had to withdraw him from college. As is so often the case, college was a topic of much anticipation for all of us, especially Max. It was an experience he had been looking forward to for years. It was his chance to get out from under our wings.

I can tell you that the first time you learn that your child is experiencing thoughts of suicide regularly, your existence as a parent changes. I went from feeling joy and hope for the future of my oldest child to an overwhelming feeling of dread and debilitating anxiety about the possibility of a much darker future. And for me, who already leaned towards anxiety in general, those years were often pure torture. Imagine that, every single day, even if everything is going relatively well, you always sense there is a storm cloud beyond the horizon. No matter how positive I tried to be, it was always there: the anxiety that at any moment we might get bad news. Maybe even the worst news possible.

Erin and I received numerous calls over the next six years that reminded us of how precarious his existence was, calls to inform us he was checking into an inpatient facility for severe depression and, yes, the dreaded suicide ideation. Every time his name appeared on my caller ID, my anxiety surged. When I called or texted him and didn't get a quick response, it was even worse.

"I can tell you that the first time you learn that your child is experiencing thoughts of suicide regularly, your existence as a parent changes."

Then there was the seizure disorder that suddenly appeared when he was 19. Now we had a new condition to worry about. It was incredibly stressful to imagine that he might be somewhere in public having a full-blown seizure or, worse, alone and injuring himself with no one to protect him.

When I reflect on those times, I don't know how I survived them, I honestly don't. I was suffering inside.

continued on next page

I occupied two worlds.

In one world, I was desperately in love with my son. I describe my love that way because I wanted so desperately for him to be happy, to be able to enjoy life, to have fun, and to just be healthy. Isn't that what every parent wants for their child? To see him in such pain was the worst experience of my life. I was fortunate, however, that as the difficult teen years, made worse by his growing depression, began to fade, some positive changes occurred in our relationship. I finally accepted that his depression was a disease and a reality he could not control. He and I finally eased into the sort of relationship we were meant to have. I simply adored him and had such affection for him. He was one of the sweetest souls I have ever known, but he was also very sarcastic and cynical, which made him even more endearing to me. I suppose I recognized a little of myself in him.

"I protected myself by hoping for the best but accepting the worst might very well happen...

However, I knew that, unlike me, who does not suffer from depression, he was going through hell much of the time. That made my love for him even more acute because I could not help him; I could only empathize with him and watch him suffer. He shared with me some very dark thoughts that were so hard to hear. I think it would be comparable to a parent whose child is in the hospital with a life-threatening disease. I felt the kind of unique, protective love only a parent can feel in those moments.

In the other world, I suffered badly. I kept it locked away, hiding it from my friends, my family, and my co-workers so I wouldn't have to talk about it. I'm good at maintaining a veneer; it is a unique gift which I have nurtured and perfected over the years. I was constantly on edge, imagining the worst could happen at any moment. Now I recognize that I went into a subconcious mode of self-protection. I protected myself by hoping for the best but accepting the worst might very well happen, thinking I would at least be prepared if it did.

That was my mental state for about the last three years before we lost him. It was painful—I don't wish it on anybody. It's the deepest kind of anxiety a person can have. It's not like the kind where one recognizes possible threats or worries; this was much deeper. And I went through it alone—yes, alone—despite a wife who would have been relieved for us to talk about it more often than we did, and friends who prayed for me and loved me but certainly couldn't really relate to my situation.

It was a journey of dread.

Yes, dread is the perfect word. So, when the moment I feared finally occurred, when I got that terrible phone call no parent ever wants to get, my first reaction was relief. Yes, that's right—relief. The monster under the bed, if you will, had finally come out and was no longer a threat. This is the only analogy I have heard that makes sense. The thing I feared most had happened, and it was suddenly behind me. It's a terrible thing to admit, and it took me almost a year to admit it to anyone other than Erin. It was not until we joined a suicide-survivor support group that I heard other parents admit to the same initial feeling. Knowing I was not alone in this may have been the most cathartic moment of my life.

But that was the only relief. The days that followed his death had their own unique journey for me emotionally. After my initial reaction that helped me survive the shock and realization that my child was gone, my emotions quickly evolved. They changed into feelings of pain, and then sadness, and then regret, and then confusion. And, of course, more anxiety.

The loss of a child is clearly a tragedy that brings tremendous pain to the parents whose hopes and wishes for their child evaporate.

To recognize "what could have been" introduces a deep sadness that is tied to all our deeply ingrained hopes from the moment our children are born.

The feeling that maybe we could have done more, or maybe we could have related to his suffering differently, becomes regret.

And then the "Why did this happen to us? Why did God allow this?" evolves into confusion.

As for the anxiety, well, I thought that would be over. It wasn't. It came out of nowhere, again. I could not understand it or control it. But with the perspective of time, I now realize why it consumed me. It was a feeling of complete loss of control. I knew more than ever that my life would not always take a predictable path, and the optimism that good things would prevail, which I enjoyed for most of my life, was gone. I felt disconnected from my foundation. Untethered, I began suffering all over again, and it just plain sucked.

With the passing of time, it has softened and eased very slowly, and I am beginning to let the need for control diminish in my life. Almost a surrender, which is a more subtle but equally impactful kind of catharsis.

"The loss of a child is clearly a tragedy that brings tremendous pain to the parents whose hopes and wishes for their child evaporate."

Thank God for Sam, and Julia.

What can I say about my youngest son, Sam? He is just an absolute joy to me. I have such deep respect and admiration for him. He is a survivor in so many ways. He was a tough little boy, a strong teenager with a great work ethic and ability to focus, and is now a pleasant and thoughtful young man who is intentional, loving, and sensitive. He had to survive the loss of his brother, the anguish of his parents, and his own pain.

He carries Max inside him in ways he may not recognize but I do: his sense of humor, his quick wit, his laugh, his sensitivity; his desire for the truth no matter how complex it may be; and his integrity. In many ways, Max's best traits were passed on to his little brother. I take comfort in that. We are so blessed because Sam found a wonderful young lady in Julia, who was a comfort to our whole family during that difficult time. I am beyond thrilled to now call her my daughter (ok, in-law, but still…). They are a joy to be around. I know Sam misses his brother, as they were very close, but thankfully he has a wonderful wife to lift him up and a group of truly devoted and intentional friends who have his back. I consider myself very lucky to have him as a son.

"In many ways, Max's best traits were passed on to his little brother. I take comfort in that."

Thank God for Erin.

To quote a good friend, I "married up." I am truly blessed to have a life partner who works intentionally to keep the relationship strong. Our marriage has always been very strong, but when the "dreaded journey" first began while Max was in college, we both handled it very differently. She made sure that we worked on staying connected and communicated well, hearing each other and respecting our differences. That hard work paid off immensely after his death. Just to be clear, she is the one who took the lead here.

Experiencing the death of a child can tear a marriage apart. While it was incredibly painful and certainly presented challenges, I believe in some ways it deepened our relationship. I love her in a way that is almost impossible to describe. I could not have gone through it without her, my wife and my best friend.

So now what?

As time continues to soften the edges of the loss and pain, as well as significantly reduce my anxiety, I have gotten much better at prioritizing what is important. It starts with the recognition that every day and every person and every experience in my life needs to be viewed with a new filter. I no longer feel that I need to live in two separate worlds.

Not every person in my life is perfect, but I get to share my ups and downs with them. I appreciate my close friends more than I ever did before this tragedy. I have also learned to forgive those who don't know what to say to me or how to best support me because there is no training or guidebook for them. They are doing their best.

"I can still find the full measure of meaning in my life, even though a part of me is gone forever.

Not every day is wonderful, but I try to make the most of each one. I can still find the full measure of meaning in my life, even though a part of me is gone forever. I know my story has not ended.

Max's story has not ended either. I think the world is a better place because of him. His legacy, captured beautifully throughout this book, has opened a lot of hearts and minds to the reality that depression is a disease like any other. He was a one-in-a-million young man. Losing him and the life he might have lived, were it not for this terrible and misunderstood disease, stings terribly even as I write this. It threatens to send me into a tailspin.

But then, the amazing love that surrounds me, from my darling wife, and my sweet Sam and Julia, and from my extended family and friends, lifts me back up. I am incredibly thankful that I have it. And I am incredibly thankful that I have Max forever in my heart.

Julia's Perspective

(Max's sister-in-law)

I remember waking up to my dad telling me Max Blechman was gone. After he said these words, I asked him to repeat himself, as if in the brief moment preceding his response, it didn't have to be true. But then he responded, his reply somehow even more unsettling: "You heard me," and he was right. Looking back, I see how in that first moment, hearing my dad's words, the trajectory of my life completely changed. I think a part of me knew it immediately.

"Looking back, I see how in that first moment, hearing my dad's words, the trajectory of my life completely changed."

The Blechmans were our neighbors, and Erin has been one of my mom's closest friends since I was little. Growing up, I knew Max to be intelligent, interesting, and talented. He was the cool, older kid at the bus stop. I knew Max, but with Sam being in my class (and the boy everyone was always trying to set me up with), he was mostly just "Sam's older brother."

A few weeks prior to Max's passing, Erin and Bill came to our house for dinner. We listened to Max's country music radio station and talked quite a bit about Max and Sam. It was casual. Every year since, a "memory" pops up on my phone of a video I took of my mom and Erin that day. I don't know what they were watching on my mom's phone, but their faces couldn't have been closer nor their guileless smiles bigger.

What once was such a lighthearted video now feels like the most ominous depiction of dramatic irony—two women I love most in this world, looking so innocent and unsuspecting, oblivious of what is to come. Watching now, I know what happens next. It was the last day we were together talking about Max in the present tense, and seeing Erin's and Bill's smiles free from impending grief. It breaks my heart to think about.

When I heard Max had passed, I pulled out my phone to text Sam and saw our most recent text exchange was a "Happy Birthday!" from Sam a few months back. Now, the text I was composing was so polar opposite. It felt as though it took an hour to come up with the words, "Sam, I am so sorry."

June 2020 consisted of daily gatherings with family and friends at the Blechmans' house. June 4th, the day after Max passed, was the first day I visited. When I walked in, Sam was sitting on the couch. I hugged him, sat beside him, and we ended up talking for hours. Most of that first conversation was about biochemistry, college, travel, and rock climbing. He seemed like Sam. At one point, I asked what he was feeling, and he briefly described feeling okay, "completely numb." We both knew he hadn't begun to process the loss. As an outsider looking in, I was so saddened to know his numbness would wear away…he lost his brother.

"I was so saddened to know his numbness would wear away… he lost his brother."

On one of those early days, Erin asked me to "please take care of Sam" and "make sure he is okay." My mom was standing beside me. It's a moment we still talk about, such a heavy, almost desperate-sounding ask, but at the time, I already knew I wanted to "be there" for Sam, whatever that meant, and so I promised Erin. I still don't know if she remembers that "ask."

For the latter half of 2020, Sam and I spent most days together. We quickly became close friends, but we didn't talk much about Max. I'd occasionally ask questions, but Sam wasn't ready to open up and, of course, I wouldn't push.

In January 2021, after a late-night climbing session, Sam asked if he could talk to me about Max. It was a tough conversation, but I felt so honored and a bit relieved that he asked. Honored because he trusted me with his feelings and his relationship with Max; relieved because I thought sharing some of his hurt would help him feel less alone.

We started dating soon after that conversation. As our relationship grew, we talked more openly about Max. Summer of 2021 is when I saw Sam's numbness begin to wear off. He seemed more distant from family and friends, less motivated at work—"lonely but not alone." He explained how the time of year, exactly one year after Max passed, was distressing. We both took time off work to travel, climb, and spend time with friends. We stayed busy. Neither of us knew exactly what this grief would look like; it seems no one truly does.

We started attending a weekly support group I found online in 2021. Those Wednesday night groups were heavy and at times draining, but more than anything, they were a way to connect with people who understood a death by suicide. Still, most people in the group had lost a child or spouse, and it was hard to watch Sam experience a loneliness that neither I nor the group could fix. Bill and Erin later joined as well, and for that group, I am forever grateful.

continued on next page

"I have learned so much about grief, loss, and how it can look so different for each person."

Over the past few years, I have learned so much about grief, loss, and how it can look so different for each person. Not that I am any sort of expert now, but I've learned a great deal since the loss of Max. As a supportive neighbor, turned best friend, turned wife, I saw how being present always trumped finding the "right" words. I have also realized that I remember much more clearly the early months following Max's passing than Sam, Erin, and Bill. Being so close to the grief seems to create a fog around everything, and the numbness Sam described to me on June 4, 2020, must have been the beginning of that fog for him. Maybe it's the mind protecting itself, or maybe grief is just so all-consuming that it simply le us aves less room for new memories.

I have walked alongside Sam in his grief while shedding a fair share of tears from what I've realized is my own grief journey. Sam and I have talked about guilt in grief—not grieving "correctly" or not feeling the "right" emotions at the "right" times. My guilt, of course, has been different than Sam's. I've felt wrong for being so upset about losing Max. After all, he wasn't MY brother or MY son. I've also really struggled with, and only recently shared, the feeling that the best thing that has ever happened to me, the love of my life, was given to me at Max's expense. If Max were still here, I might not have my Sam. I know that Max's family does not share this perspective, but it is something I wanted to share in case anyone may someday need to hear it.

More than grief I have learned about love, which I suppose is what makes grief so intense. I have been so fortunate to become a part of Sam's family. I love Sam. I love Erin and Bill. I love Max.

Sam and I were married in December 2023. I've thought a lot about how that makes Max my brother now, too. I was lucky to know Max for the time I did, and I also realize that I know him so much better now than I did when he was actually here. I love him, I miss him, I wish I could hug him. As heavy as it is, I'm glad I feel that way; it means having a piece of Max with me. I now have the honor of carrying on his memory alongside Sam. The cool, older neighbor-boy that I once described as "Sam's big brother" is now mine, too.

"Sam and I were married in December 2023. I've thought a lot about how that makes Max my brother now, too."

Sam's Perspective (Max's younger brother)

"Max was so much more than a brother to me...he was my mentor, my protector, & my companion."

Losing my older brother Max is by far the most challenging experience I have ever dealt with. My grief journey has involved a complex mixture of thoughts and emotions. There are moments of despair, hopelessness, and confusion. There are moments of nostalgia, longing, and pain. There are moments of numbness, followed by guilt for not feeling anything at all. Although my emotions changed over time, I can be sure there will always be a tumultuous mix.

Max was so much more than a brother to me; he helped shape me into the person I am today. At times he was my mentor, my protector, and my companion. Early in our lives, I served merely to annoy Max. In later years, we grew close and began to share our lives together. Unfortunately, our relationship was cut short due to his death. I will forever regret the aspects of my life that are no longer because of his absence. He was not the best man at my wedding. He will not see me finish graduate school and start my career. He will not be there to offer me guidance throughout the rest of my life. My children will not have his children to play with and grow up alongside. He will never call me "nerd" or "dork" again. We will not spend holidays together. The list goes on and on.

continued on next page

"*He will not see me finish graduate school and start my career. My children will not have his children to play with …He will never call me "nerd" or "dork" again.*

I learned from Max several key components of my worldview. I cherish the thought that pieces of him live on in me. Since his death, I have struggled to adjust to a world without him. For my whole life, I had Max to look to in times of confusion. Max had a (fairly) well-informed opinion about most things, and as an inquisitive person I turned to him as the source of many truths. From the outside it may seem secondary to my grief journey, but forging a path on my own has not been easy without my wise and knowledgeable older brother. Occasionally, I find comfort in knowing that he would be proud of me and my trajectory as a young man. However, I often feel lost and wonder, "What would Max have thought or said or done?"

Max's amazing qualities make his loss even more painful. He could fill a room with immense joy and laughter and talk endlessly about philosophy and politics. The number of people who, after Max's death, spoke or posted online about the positive impact he had on their life is staggering. He was charismatic, charming, and fun loving. He was compassionate, convicted, and caring. He was funny, serious, and smart. His life was also full of pain, fear, and suffering, as he battled depression, anxiety, and physical health problems for many years. I was largely shielded from the depths of his despair, perhaps because of our parents' efforts to protect me, along with my own ignorance, which caused me to be blind to his situation. I look back and wish I could have been there for him during those times, but I understand this is something I cannot change.

I view my life as being on either side of the loss of Max: before and after. I often struggle to connect the two "halves" due to their immense differences. Any darkness I experienced before losing Max does not compare to what I have experienced since. Interestingly, though, the four years since Max's death have also been filled with much joy and many meaningful experiences. Some of the positive life changes have occurred *despite* Max's death. However, one amazing thing occurred *because of* his loss: my relationship with my incredible wife, Julia. She is a bright light in this dark world. Though I had known Julia for many years, she properly stepped into my life the very same day Max left it. During our wedding in December 2023, our close friends and family pointed out how they felt that Max had put Julia in my life on purpose. I am forever grateful we have each other, and, in part, I have Max to thank for that.

"*Though I had known Julia for many years, she properly stepped into my life the very same day Max left it.*"

I am also grateful to my wonderful mom, who in this book captures Max's essence, illness, and pain. She tells many sweet and compelling stories from his childhood, adolescence, and adulthood. She also provides a raw and unfiltered peek into the depths of her pain in the days, months, and years after his death. I relate to many of the thoughts expressed throughout the book, but I also recognize that differences in our grief journeys are to be expected. Although I miss Max deeply, I cherish the impact he has had on me. I strive to carry forward his legacy and show the world a fraction of his strength, resilience, and spirit.

My Perspective

It's been four years since we lost our beloved Max. It's hard to believe it's been that long, and yet in some ways it feels as if it has been much longer. I've learned this is the way grief works: it distorts time and drastically alters our perspective.

I've learned so much about grief over the past four years. To say surviving Max's death has been the most devastating and difficult experience of my life feels like a massive understatement. Following his death, I felt desperate, depressed, and hopeless for so long that I honestly thought there was something seriously wrong with me, like I needed to be committed to some institution because I felt unfit for regular society. That sounds like hyperbole, but it's honestly not.

"I've learned this is the way grief works: it distorts time and drastically alters our perspective.

"I honestly think the loss of a child is in a category all by itself."

As I learned about grief, I began to understand and accept that I was feeling the normal and natural reactions of losing someone so special, and that losing a child is unfathomable. My beautiful mother also passed away during these four years since we lost Max, and I can say with certainty that although her death has been sad, it is nothing like losing our Max. When an elderly parent passes, we usually don't feel grief over our lost hopes and dreams for them like we do when we lose a child. I won't compare grief because our personal grief is the worst, but I honestly think the loss of a child is in a category all by itself. Since Max passed, I've become an author. I've written and released this book, which has allowed me to connect with other parents who have suffered the tragic and traumatic loss of a child, or who fear such a loss from mental illness. It has been an honor to hear their stories and share their grief.

I've become a grief educator to help other parents navigate their own debilitating loss because the early days of grief are intense, overwhelming, and all-encompassing. My grief support groups are helpful and healing for me and so gratifying as I watch the way participants bond together to support and encourage one another. Support groups help to normalize our experience and validate our thoughts and feelings, which is so critical when we are grieving.

I've become a speaker to help educate and raise awareness about mental illness, suicide, loss, and grief. We need to talk more openly about these difficult, yet often taboo, topics, so we can remove the stigma and increase compassion.

According to grief expert David Kessler, the sixth stage of grief is **meaning**—finding meaning again in your life following a loss. My meaning, or purpose as I think of it, is to elevate the conversation about the difficult topics of mental illness, suicide, loss, and grief. My purpose is to help other parents realize that surviving their child's death is possible. My purpose is to educate others about grief in order to support those who lose a loved one. My purpose is to help people who are grieving feel less alone and broken. My purpose is to honor my sweet Max.

"My purpose is to help other parents realize that surviving their child's death is possible... to educate others about grief in order to support those who lose a loved one...to help people who are grieving feel less alone and broken. My purpose is to honor my sweet Max."

Four years later, our family looks different. Although we no longer have our beloved Max, we have gained a beautiful daughter in Julia, whom Sam married in December 2023. She came into Sam's life immediately following Max's death, and she's been his rock ever since. I honestly believe Max brought Sam and Julia together. He knew that, in his absence, Sam needed a confidant and a best friend. He knew that Sam needed someone to offer him encouragement, unconditional love, and admiration—all the things that Max gave to Sam. He knew that Sam was going to need someone with grit, wisdom, maturity, kindness, and loyalty to help him navigate this devastating loss. And so, I believe, that from Heaven, Max brought beautiful Julia into Sam's life and orchestrated their

"And so, I believe, that from Heaven, Max brought beautiful Julia into Sam's life & orchestrated their once-in-a-lifetime love."

once-in-a-lifetime love. We couldn't be happier that Sam has an amazing life partner, and Bill and I have a lovely new daughter. As a Jesus follower, the past four years have required me to re-evaluate my faith. I honestly believed that God owed me something because I prayed fervently and faithfully for Max for so many years. The anger and abandonment I felt were the result of faulty theology on my part. In hindsight, I now realize God never actually abandoned me: He was with me all along. He was not irritated or even surprised by my anger, but rather waited patiently for me to turn back to Him as He gently and slowly restored and renewed my hope and faith.

The following bible verse sums things up:

"Sing for joy…. For the Lord has comforted His people and will have compassion on them in their suffering." Isaiah 49:13 If you are in the throes of a deep, dark grief, please remember that God is close to you, even if you don't feel Him. He WILL comfort you and have compassion on you in your suffering.

"He gently and slowly restored and renewed my hope and faith."

BIBLIOGRAPHY

1. Moore, Beth. *Daniel: Lives of Integrity, Words of Prophecy*. Nashville, TN: Lifeway Press, 2006.
2. *Man vs. Wild*, starring Bear Grylls. Discovery Channel, 2006-2011. Television.
3. Kari Jobe & Codi Carnes live from Elevation Ballantyne. "The Blessing, 2020." YouTube, https://bitly/2kzs91K.
4. Stephens, Paula., M.A. RYT-200. *What I Wish Other People Understood About Losing a Child*. February 13, 2020, https://www.mindbodygreen.com/0-17928/what-i-wish-more-people-understood-about-losing-a-child.html
5. Van der Kolk, Bessel. *The Body Keeps the Score: Brain, Mind, and Body in the Healing of Trauma*. NY: Penguin Books, 2014.
6. Cacciatore, Joanne, Dr. *A Bed for My Heart*. November 6, 2019, https://www.facebook.com/ABedForMyHeart/posts/963605553810344.
7. Guinan, Michael D. OFM, "Biblical Lament: Prayer out of Pain." Franciscan Spirit (blog), Accessed October 2020, https://www.franciscanmedia.org/franciscan-spirit-blog/biblical-laments-prayer-out-of-pain.
8. Paul, Guest post. "Divorce Rates—And Can Marriage Really Survive the Loss of a Child." *Standing Still Magazine*, June 2016, Stillstandmag.com.
9. *The Lion King*. Dir. Rob Minkoff, Roger Allers. Perf. James Earl Jones, Jeremy Irons, Jonathan Taylor Thomas. Walt Disney Pictures: 1994, VHS.
10. Stoecklein, Kayla. *Fear Gone Wild, A Story of Mental Illness, Suicide, and Hope Through Loss*. Nashville: Thomas Nelson Publishing, 2020.
11. Klune, T.J. *The House in the Cerulean Sea*. New York: Tor Books, 2020.
12. Rowling, J.K, *Harry Potter and the Philosopher's Stone*. UK: Bloomsbury, 1997.
13. Paolini, Christopher. *The Inheritance Cycle*. NY: Knopf Doubleday Publishing, 2002-2011.
14. Coxe, Molly. *Cat Traps*. New York: Random House Books, 1995.
15. Karpinski Ruth I, [et al.] "High Intelligence: A Risk Factor for Psychological and Physiological Overexcitabilities." *Intelligence Advance* online publication. September 2017, https://doi.org/10.1016/j.intell.2017.09.
16. Page, Rick. *Hope is Not a Strategy: The 6 Keys to Winning the Complex Sale*. N.Y.: Nautilus Press, 2001.
17. Norful, Smokie. "I Understand." BMI, 2012. Accessed February 20, 2021, https://youtu.be/l0skD7d3usw.
18. Obama, Michelle. *Becoming*. New York: Crown Publishing, 2018.
19. Laditan, Bunmi. *Dear God: Honest Prayers to a God Who Listens*. Grand Rapids: Zondervan, 2021, p. 120.
20. Royston, Angela. *Diggers and Dump Trucks*. New York: Little Simon. 1991.
21. Amanda Fialk. "Cops shouldn't be the first at scene in mental health crisis." *USA Today*, December 2, 2020. Cops shouldn't be first at mental health call. NYC program needed nationwide. (usatoday.com).
22. Ranna Parekh, M.D., M.P.H. "Warning Signs of Mental Illness." *American Psychiatric Association Website*, July 2018, https://www.psychiatry.org/patients-families/warning-signs-of-mental-illness.

23. Jaimie Rosenberg. "Mental Health Issues on the Rise Among Adolescents, Young Adults." *American Journal of Managed Care Website*, March 19, 2019, https://www.ajmc.com/view/mental-health-issues-on-the-rise-among-adolescents-young-adults.

24. Ashley Hamer, "Here's Why Smells Trigger Such Vivid Memories." *Discovery Website*, August 1, 2019, https://www.discovery.com/science/Why-Smells-Trigger-Such-Vivid-Memories.

25. Cacciatore, Joanne, Dr. "Mother's Day is for Grieving Mothers, too." *Center for Loss and Trauma Website*, July 18, 2020, https://www.centerforlossandtrauma.com/post/mother-s-day-is-for-grieving-mothers-too.

26. Dunn, Bill and Leonard, Kathy. *Through a Season of Grief: Devotions for Your Journey from Mourning to Joy*. Nashville: Thomas Nelson, Inc., 2004, Remembering Good Memories, p. 364.

27. *Through a Season of Grief*, p. 358.

28. Morlin, Amy. "Seven Subtle Signs of Depression You Shouldn't Ignore: Depression Isn't Just About Feeling Sad." Inc.com website, October 6, 201., https://www.inc.com/amy-morin/7-subtle-signs-of-depression-you-shouldn-t-ignore.html.

29. Rickman, Alan, Dir. *A Little Chaos*. London: Artemis and BBC Films, 2014.

30. Quinn, Kate. *The Rose Code*. N.Y.: Harper Collins, 2021, p. 285.

31. "Grieving the Death of a Child," taken from Healinggrief.org website, https://healgrief.org/grieving-the-death-of-a-child/.

32. *Through a Season of Grief*, Through a Season of Communicating in Grief, p. 356.

33. "Complicated Grief," taken from mayoclinic.org website, https://www.mayoclinic.org/diseases-conditions/complicated-grief/symptoms-causes/syc-20360374f.

34. Steel, Danielle. *His Bright Light, The Story of Nick Traina*. New York: Dell Publishing, 1998, pp. Prologue x and xxi.

35. Curtin, Sally C., M.A. and Heron, Melonie, Ph.D. "Death Rates Due to Suicide and Homicide Among Persons Aged 10–24". United States: 2000–2017. NCHS Data Brief, No. 3552, October 2019, https://www.cdc.gov/nchs/data/databriefs/db352-h.pdf.

36. Devine, Megan. *It's Okay That You're Not Okay*. Louisville, CO: Sounds True Publishing, 2017.

37. Burpo, Todd. *Heaven Is for Real*. Nashville, TN: Thomas Nelson, 1940.

38. Haynes, Natalie. *A Thousand Ships*. New York: Harper Collins, 2021, p. 222.

39. *It's Okay That You're Not Okay*. pp. 157, 160, 161.

40. Murkoff, Heidi. *What to Expect When You're Expecting*. N.Y.: Workman Publishing Company, 1984.

41. Bowler, Kate. *No Cure for Being Human (And Other Truths I Needed to Hear)*. New York: Random House, 2021, pp. 188, 155.

42. Dave, Laura. *The Last Thing He Told Me*. NY: Simon & Schuster, 2021.

43. Munsch, Robert. *Love You Forever*. Illustrated by Sheila McGraw. Richmond Hill, ON, Canada: Firefly Books, 1986.

A Bird Named "Heaven"

"Erin's authentic and passionate entries about her journey immediately following her son's passing touched a deep part of my soul. When I read her entry about the twigs falling amid emotions of anger—then, a little, joyful bird appearing, chills ran up my arms, and I knew the bird was a whisper of God. In this broken world, where suffering and despair can grip our lives after such traumas, God's tiny, perfect creations provide glistening hope. I pray the vibrant colors, energetic movement, and gentleness of this bird have inspired some whispers of hope through your experience of Erin's book."

- Sarah Nelsen, illustrator & graphic designer

Sarah Teresa Nelsen has a personal connection with suicide awareness and prevention. Through her business, Atlas Art, she has ongoing partnerships with the American Foundation for Suicide Prevention to provide custom art kits and creative, therapeutic activities for survivors of suicide. She also works with organizations focused on empowerment and recovery for Survivors of Human Trafficking, Homelessness, and Loss.

Nelsen is greatly inspired by the process of creating something outside yourself and has witnessed how it improves mental health, confidence, and calm. As the 2020 pandemic faded, she opened Atlas Art studio, a space for people to "*Unwind. Connect. Navigate Life Creatively.*" Her products and workshops have helped people find beauty within this messy life. Her work and mission is fueled by God's word, leaps of faith, unedited prayer, and most of all—real life experiences.

Nelsen holds a B.A. in Graphic Design and Integrative Arts from Pennsylvania State University. She lives in Pittsburgh, PA, with her husband, two daughters, and two rescue pups. You can find Sarah's cards, art, writings, and other inspiring products online at AtlasArtLove.com.

VISIT: ATLASARTLOVE.COM | **FOLLOW:** @ATLASARTLOVE

HEAVEN IS HAPPINESS
Watercolor & Charcoal, 2022.

BEAUTIFUL BROWN EYES
Watercolor & Charcoal, 2022.

WITHIN REACH
Watercolor & Charcoal, 2022.

PEACE BE STILL
Watercolor & Charcoal, 2022.

PERFECT LOVE
Watercolor & Charcoal, 2022.

ALWAYS WITH YOU
Watercolor & Charcoal, 2022.

in gratitude

I would like to thank the many people who helped this book come to fruition. Julie Boynton, my copyeditor, proofreader, and soul sister; words cannot even begin to describe your contribution. Thank you from the bottom of my heart. Sarah Nelsen, my tremendously talented designer, and illustrator, it was like you got inside my head to bring to life the beauty I envisioned for this book. Valerie Shannon, Gina Bolton, Adam Jackley, Noriene Schmit, and Tina Dollard, thank you for your feedback, suggestions, encouragement, and support. To my wonderful husband, Bill, and amazing son, Sam, your ongoing love and support have been invaluable, you make life worth living. Thank you for the strength you've provided to me since losing our Max.

To my precious, Max, I always thought you would be the one to write a book. Although you left this earth way too soon, your brief life had a great impact on me and taught me much. Thank you for the multitude of experiences and memories to draw from. Words cannot express my love for you and my pride in being your mom. It is one of the greatest gifts of my life.

about the author

Erin Blechman knows firsthand the difficulty of dealing with a child who struggles with mental and physical illness. As a wife and mother whose family is most important, *My Unexpected Journey* chronicles the eighteen months following the devastating loss of her beloved son, Max, to suicide.

She hopes to bring compassion and understanding to mental illness, suicide, loss, and grief. She lives part-time in both Pittsburgh, Pennsylvania and Naples, Florida with her husband, Bill. Her son, Sam, resides in Pittsburgh. *My Unexpected Journey* is her first book.

HELPFUL RESOURCES

American Foundation for Suicide Prevention

AFSP.ORG
800-273-8255 or text "TALK" to 741741

AFSP's mission is to save lives and bring hope to those affected by suicide. It is a voluntary health organization that gives those affected by suicide a nationwide community empowered by research, education and advocacy to take action against this leading cause of death.

Crisis Text Line

crisistextline.org
Text this phone number: 741741

Crisis Text Line provides free, 24/7, high-quality text-based mental health support and crisis intervention by empowering a community of trained volunteers to support people in their moments of need.

National Alliance on Mental Illness (NAMI)

NAMI.ORG
Helpline: 1-800-950-6264

NAMI's mission is to provide advocacy, education, support and public awareness so that all individuals and families affected by mental illness can build better lives.

988 Suicide and Crisis Lifeline

suicidepreventionlifeline.org
Call or text 988

The 988 Lifeline is available 24/7/365. Conversations are free and confidential.

In Honor of

MAXWELL ALEXANDER BLECHMAN

September 29, 1994 –June 03, 2020

www.ingramcontent.com/pod-product-compliance
Ingram Content Group UK Ltd.
Pitfield, Milton Keynes, MK11 3LW, UK
UKHW050146280726
14058UKWH00007B/851

9 798218 544393